Face, Assess, and Address Your Truths

"A 3 Step Self-Help Book to Assist Adults in Finding the Ability to Heal, Move Past Your Past, and to Move Forward with Your Life, by Starting Over"

Doneareum S. Winston

Published in the United States of America

ISBN 978-1-960684-08-0 (SC)
ISBN 978-1-960684-07-3 (Ebook)

Doneareum S. Winston Publishing
222 West 6th Street
Suite 400, San Pedro, CA, 90731
doneareumw@yahoo.com

Order Information and Rights Permission:

Quantity sales. Special discounts might be available on quantity purchases by corporations, associations, and others. For details, contact the publisher at the address above.

For Book Rights Adaptation and other Rights Permission.
Call us at toll-free 1-888-945-8513 or send us an email at
admin@stellarliterary.com.

Contents

Chapter 1
Finding your Ability to Heal, Start Over, and Move Forward with your Life

"Life would have been entirely different for me; if I could have just, started over. I may not be where I am today; if I had done things, differently. I may have a better relationship with my children, if I had done this. I probably would still be married, if I had done that. I would be in a better predicament financially, if I never would have made that mistake. I wish I could change the past. I just wish we could start over. If only I had never met this person; then I wouldn't be in this predicament. I know it's too late for me; so I guess I'll just have to live with it. I wish I had never gone through that. The time I lost with my family wouldn't be so great; if I wouldn't have done, or said this. I don't know why I had to lead the life I led; but I wish things would've worked out differently, for me. I should've, could've, would've………… if only."

Do you ever find yourself thinking these thoughts, or feeling this way? Perhaps you know someone that does? So my question to you is; is it ever too late to start over after it's all said, and done?

For many of us, we feel as though the damage has been done. It's too late. It doesn't matter anymore. I can't change the past; or the way things were. We grow older, wiser through our experiences, and encounters. We look back just to question how things may have worked out, if only. Why? Why do we have to question and dwell upon our failures, past faults, and misdeeds in life? Is it human nature? Is it in us to feel some type of guilt; and to drown within our sorrows for actions taken, words spoken, or left unsaid? Is it in us to just give up; and to continue to let it be, as opposed to making a change for the better? **Will we ever be able to right our wrongs, in the eyes of others?** Can we ever truly heal? Can we let go of all the situations that occurred within our yesterday; in order to lead a better life, in our today? Why is it so hard to start over wholeheartedly, and sincerely? Let's look at a few scenarios:

1

Scenario1- (Behind closed doors; a father who was not there for his son, feels remorseful. He harbors an inner guilt, for not being present within his son's life when he was a child. The child endured a lot of hardships; yet he overcame his adversities. The son reached out to his father to establish some type of relationship. The father tries to establish something of tangible value; but it is difficult for him to do so. The father has his own inner issues that he has yet to deal with, in regards to his relationship with his own father. Life continues to pass, and the father and son seldom communicate. A real bond has yet to be established. The son at times, feels as though his father is wrong for not trying wholeheartedly; and sincerely to establish, a connection. The father feels at times, that the son is wrong; because even though he was not present, he feels that the son should view him in a "fatherly light." Distance continues to grow, and time continues to pass. In the back of the father's mind, he feels that he is justified for not reaching out; because too much time has passed. The father knows how he would honestly feel within his own mind, if he were the son. The son continues to move on with his life, in spite of. **What is wrong with this picture? How often do we see this type of father and son relationship within, society? Is it ever too late for them to start over, and get to know each other? Will a difference in perspective always remain? Why? How can this relationship be mended? What will it take to move forward for both of these men?**)

Scenario 2- (Behind closed doors, a young mother has 2 children. She doesn't know much about the fathers; for she only knew them briefly enough, to create the children. The young mother parties often; and views her friendships to be more important, than raising her children. Due to her reckless, inconsiderate, and unhealthy lifestyle; she is incapable of raising her children. A relative steps forwards to take them in. The young mother seldom visits, calls, nor provides anything for her children. When she does come around she is under the influence of alcohol, and drugs. The relative eventually tells her that she is no longer welcome to come around their home. The 2 children grow up sheltered from their own mother; and move on with their lives. In her old age, the mother has now become settled; and seeks to establish a relationship with her 2 children, and grandchildren. The children are bitter, and hostile towards her. The children bitterly; and angrily address her when she tries to tell them that, she is sorry. She wishes that she had done better by them. The old woman now leads a life of sadness in solitude; for she regrets her actions in not doing right, by her children. The now adult children could care less; for they learned to live, found peace, and happiness without her in their lives. They have no interest in getting to know their mother. **Does this happen within society, today? Are the children wrong for disowning their mother; although she wasn't there for them, when they were little? Is the mother at fault for wanting to reach out; and establish a relationship, now that she has matured? Is anyone at fault; or is everyone justified in their behavior, and way of thinking? Is it too late to start over for this family?**)

Scenario3- (Behind closed doors, an elder couple is burglarized; and robbed of their possessions by an armed, and masked man. They call the police to file a report. They eventually go to the police station to identify the man that did this to them. Although they could not visibly see the whole face of the man; they claim to recall the look within his eyes, and the shape of his mouth. They identify a man who is blamed for the crime; although it is the wrong man. A wrongfully accused man pleads his innocence; yet he still ends up doing time for a crime that he did not commit. The man serves his time and is released from prison. He goes on to become an advocate for the wrongfully accused. He often shares his story; and how it did not keep him from wanting to pursue, a normal life. The elder couple; often wonder if they made a mistake by picking out, the wrong man. They go to 1 of the man's speaking engagements within their community. Afterwards, the couple approaches the man to apologize. They ask for his forgiveness. They feel remorseful. The man tells the couple that he can't forgive them for the damage they caused to his life. He is still bitter, and resentful for having to serve time for a crime that he did not commit. The elder couple leaves in disappointment. They are glad to have been able to at least apologize to the man for their mistake. **How often do we see, read, and hear about cases such as this? Is the man wrong for not being willing to accept the couple's apology? Were they wrong to identify**

him within the line-up; although they were not sure? Is it too late to let go; and forgive, the past? Is it too late to move on, and start over?)

Our truth is that no matter what occurs within our lives for better, or for worse; it occurs. It happened. Do we get the desired results in terms of closure that we seek; in most cases, no. Although we try to heal, move forward, and to understand why things begin or end the way they do; we do not get the closure that we felt that we deserve. We do not always hear the apologies, receive the forgiveness, find the compromise; nor the balance that we feel that we need.

We reach out to establish something of value, put our pride aside, and attempt to move forward; regardless of what occurs, is said, or done. This affects us emotionally, and mentally. **Some of us take responsibility for the actions taken; or words spoken that may have harmed, or hurt others. We do not always get this same accountability from others in return.** So what does this mean? It means that no matter how right you feel that you are in regards to any situation or circumstance; others may not necessarily agree. Everyone will not be prepared to face their truths, find closure, forgive, and heal when you are. So what do you do?

Your "truth" sets you free. That doesn't mean that it will free someone else. We may never fully understand; why others think, and feel the way that they do. Why they hold onto the specific belief systems, principles; and standards that they do, regardless of how this may affect others. Does this mean that we must wage a constant battle; or struggle with others, since we do not fully understand, nor comprehend their motives? No. It means that your healing is your own; and for your own benefit, within your own allotted time frame. **You can desire to seek peaceful communications; and interactions with everyone that you come into contact with, but will this mean that you will get the same in return? We are all human beings. We have the freedom, and the right to be who we want to be in thought and in action; for better, or for worse.**

When we are children we are not responsible; nor accountable for some things done to us. We can't help our conditions, and circumstances. We look for guidance, help, nurturing, love, and support from those responsible for us. Did all of us receive just this; of course not. Does it still affect our minds and hearts today when we recount our pasts? Yes. Are we ever justified in feeling a certain type of way because; of what was done or said, to us as children?

As adults we become accountable; and responsible for our own actions, and the words we speak unto others. We decide, and control whether or not we will say or do something hurtful; or harmful to one another. When we are young, and learning the ways of the world; we often act, and speak without thinking things through thoroughly. We tend to not pay close attention to the affects that our actions have upon not just our lives; but the lives of others. Is it because we don't care; or can we use the excuse that according to our upbringing, we just don't know any better. So when do we learn to do, and become better? When do we decide, and determine to make things right for ourselves; as well as those who surround us?

We decide to Heal, move forward; and to start over when we are able to allow ourselves to be released from the circumstances, burdens, barriers, poisons, and issues that have an impact upon our lives in a negative sense. A former drug addict, alcoholic, criminal, smoker, prisoner, or anyone who suffered from an issue that controlled their life; because it was greater than them, will tell you that the day they looked at themselves for who they really were is when they saw the error of their ways. They realized that they were in control, and determined the outcome of their life. Was it a challenge? Was it difficult to stop trying to escape their reality through the drugs, crime, sin, and the alcohol; of course! Why? They had surrendered to the negativity within their lives. They had become dependent upon that negative coping mechanism; which in turn caused them to face, an inner battle.

Each time that they were reminded of the pain, the hurt, the suffering, the loss, the challenge, and the reason why they sought that specific escape route to begin with; they regressed. **They stopped forward progress and went backwards; regardless of how far they had come, and how good they were doing without needing to escape. Letting go is hard.** Why; because we can't change our pasts. However, we can always start over despite our background, age, and circumstances. We can break the chains that bind us.

We can open doors that were once closed. We can arrive to our desired destination.

Do not only ask, and reach out; but allow someone to help you. There are those who want to see you succeed; because they once had to walk a mile in your shoes. There are those who are compassionate, kind, caring, and considerate enough to be willing to sacrifice what they have, share what they know; and give their last, in order to help you. The question is, "Are you willing to help yourself? Are you ready to let go, and move on?"

We often fear the unknown, and starting over can be questionable. What if this happens? What if that happens? What if this or that doesn't? What will I do? How will I maintain, or make it through? What if they don't receive, accept; or give what I'm ready to offer, or need? No one wants to look like a fool; or to be told "that was a dumb decision, or stupid mistake." We all seek validation; and the approval of others at some point, in time. We all desire that pat on the back. We need to receive cheers; and accolades from a job, well done. Some chances are worth taking while some decisions, are worth putting on hold. Ultimately, you are the 1 who decides what will; or will not work for you.

You decide when it is time to make a change, for the better. You decide when to move forward. "Patience," can be a challenge; because we tend to want what we want, when we want it. We want the money, homes, cars, clothes, jewelry, relationship, family, and friendships that will make us happy. Many of us are seldom willing to patiently wait on the timeframe that will allow these things to come into fruition. So how do we time things, just right? Is it possible to do so? Some people believe that what you desire most in life will occur, when it is time for it to. There are times when we have to grow in order to become mature, responsible, and wise enough to be appreciative.

1 of the most important things that I have learned about life is to simply live it. Learn valuable lessons from your struggles, faults, challenges, hardships, and adversities. Laugh when you feel like crying; because sometimes the pain is too much to bear. Find the humor in the things that you take too seriously, and over stress about. Love the people you encounter for better or for worse; because they help you grow. **The good people within**

6

your life remind you that this world isn't such a bad place. **The bad people in your life should always show you, who you do not want to become.**

Behind closed doors, we all have to endure some form of strife that others will not know, or see. We all have had something occur within our lives that possibly affected us for better; or for worse in our outlook on the people, places, and things that play a role within our daily lives. Know that you are not the only 1 who has to raise a child alone, battling addiction, struggling financially, being lied to, cheated on, mistreated, abused, let down, struggling, and suffering. You are not alone; and if the burdens are too much to bear, then do not be afraid to speak out Let your voice be heard, as well as your Prayers answered.

Our sufferings are often prolonged; because we are reluctant, to release. We are hesitant to seek help; because we fear what may happen for the worse, embarrassment, humiliation, vengeance, retaliation, sadness, hurt, and the pain that it will cause. However, you can't; and must not be afraid to free, yourself. Do not fear consequence for the truth always prevails; and there is Healing within, the truth. You must be willing to embrace your truth at some point in time; in order to start over, and to move past, the past.

You will endure the hardships, challenges, and adversities that you face. You will come out in the end, victorious. Strive to continue your forward progress. Do not be afraid to look back; and to reach out in order to help someone else trying to overcome. **Realize that the only direction that you are choosing to move in is forward. Progress, is always a good thing.**

Avoid the people, places, and things that have anchored you down for the worse, in a negative sense. Let go of the drugs, alcohol, and the negative thinkers who tell you that you are nothing. You are not stupid. You desire to change for the better; as well as to, heal. Focus on taking care of your responsibilities, loved ones, and most importantly yourself; because if you can't help you, then you can't help anyone else. **Do not fear facing, assessing, and addressing your truths in order to embrace the healing,** within. Leave your past within the past, and move towards your greater self. Know that you are imperfect, will make mistakes, have challenges, and adversities to overcome along the way. Learn lessons from the mistakes, faults, and shortcomings that you may have, or make. Walk within the knowledge of leaving behind your lesser self; so that you may become, your greater self. You may now open the doors that were once closed before you; for you no longer need to hide, behind them.

Chapter 2
Issues and Problems with Other People

"I can't stand that person; because they are always up to something, and that something is probably no good! Every time that I try to do better; this person always goes out of their way, to give me a hard time! I get sick, and tired of hearing about; and trying to help you with your issues! You have Problems! There are days when I can't bring myself to go to work; because of the issues that I have, with certain people there. I am tired of trying to work through our issues, within this relationship. It doesn't matter how hard I try; nothing seems to be good enough, for that person. People keep telling me that person is talking negatively about me; and I'm ready, to confront them! I don't want to help you; because you don't help me, when I need it. I'm tired of people telling me that I'm crazy; because they don't understand, what I'm telling them."

Have you ever heard, or stated any of these statements? Do you ever state any of this to, toward, or about someone else? Did someone tell you any of this about someone else? Why? Are these statements made out of jealousy, bitterness, resentment, and other inner issues; that we have yet to address within, our own lives? Do we sometimes find ourselves playing the "blame game," when it comes to dealing with our problems with others? Why is it so difficult to face, assess, and address our inner; or outer truths in order to embrace the healing, within a specific situation? Let's look at a couple of scenarios:

Scenario 1- (Behind closed doors, a young man who has recently graduated from high school is searching for a job. He does not want to attend college. He has a hard time finding a decent paying job; until 1 day, he does. He starts the new job. Soon after, he seeks to make friends on the job. He does not fit in with the other people who have worked the job for years; and so they ridicule him. They laugh at him, and talk about him when he makes mistakes, on the job. Neither of his co-workers try to help him; nor correct him, when he makes mistakes. They constantly ask him, if he is going to quit the job. The young man feels saddened by the fact that his co-workers do not seem to be supportive of him wanting to work with them. He feels that he has no one to talk to about his issues; because even the supervisor, tends to ridicule him. The supervisor addresses him harshly when, he asks for help with his tasks. The young man sits alone during breaks at the job. He dwells upon the negativity that surrounds him; but he does not quit the job. He knows that decent jobs are hard to come by. He has personal problems within his home life that no one else knows about. 1 day he is on the job being ridiculed, when he loses control. He confronts 1 of his co-workers; and they get into a fight! The co-worker denies that he has been harassing, and ridiculing the new worker. The company fires the new worker. **Does this happen often within our society today? Why do you think the co-workers ridiculed; and did not want to befriend, the young man? Do you think the young man should have pursued college, instead? Is it too late for him to start over? What could have occurred, that would have made a difference in the outcome of this scenario? Does the young man have issues?**)

Scenario 2- (Behind closed doors, a woman endures a challenging life. She grew up within poverty. She was raised within a single- parent household. She is shy, and keeps to herself. She overcomes her adversities; and gains a college degree in order to pursue, a chosen career path. She gets the job that she desires. On her job, she has people that like to pry into the personal affairs of others. They enjoy gossip. She does not engage within this behavior, and keeps to herself. She is a hard and diligent worker; and is career, and goal-oriented. 1 day, a new worker starts the job. The new worker knows this young woman. They grew up within the same neighborhood. The new worker tells her co-workers what she knows about the young woman that keeps to herself. She gossips about the woman's family life, their struggle to endure and overcome conditions of poverty, her failed attempts at relationships, spreads rumors, and lies about her sexual orientation. The new worker does this to fit in; and to make friends, on the job. The co-workers begin to harass, ridicule, and make hurtful comments and remarks toward her. The young woman is confused as to where they gathered this information; because she did not share it. 1 day out of frustration, she loses her cool; and confronts the new worker, in front of their co-workers! The new worker is ashamed; and feels bad about what she said, to fit in. The co-workers now laugh at; and ridicule the new worker, while they call the other young woman "crazy." The new worker eventually quits the job. **Does this happen within our society today? Why do people say; and do negative things to fit in, amongst their peers? Was the young woman who kept to herself, wrong for losing her cool? Are the coworkers at fault for their immature behavior, upon the job? Should the new worker have shared the young woman's private life upon the job? What could have occurred to affect the outcome of this scenario, in a more positive way?**)

Who hasn't had an issue with someone, as of late? Who hasn't been talked down on by their co-workers, bosses, friends, family; or the people within their community, for some odd reason? So how did you deal with it? Did you tactfully confront the person, and the issue? Did you blow up, start cursing, handing out threats, and taking names? Did you just ignore the problems; and now they are slowly but surely eating at you? This is all because you have yet, to deal with them? Well……………..

You do not; and will not fit in everywhere you go, amongst all the people that you encounter. Why? Is it because of our personal beliefs, differences, values, principles, mentalities, and the ideals that we stand firmly upon? Why is it that when these belief systems are challenged; and the status quo is interrupted, then chaos and confusion ensue?

Logically, we all want to get along with everyone. We want to make friends, have fun, live, and enjoy healthy lifestyles. So how do we deal with the issues; and problems that we have, with other people? How do we cope in a healthy and productive manner? It is important to figure out, why there is a problem to begin with?

Some people don't like the way you look, smell, act, behave, think, and just plain; and simple, the individual that you are. In many cases, these prejudices derive from not only cultural; but learned behaviors. If you

11

are dogmatically taught as a child not to like a certain type of race, culture, person, place; or thing, then chances are very likely that as you grow older, this dislike, disdain, and ignorance, will grow within you as well. **The sad fact is that you honestly probably don't even logically know why you don't like whom; or whatever for whatever reason, outside this is what you were taught.** This mentality; or bizarre belief system, is all you know. "They don't come from where I come from, have what I have, know what I know, endure what I endure, struggle the way I do, think the way I do, or see things the way I do; so they just don't understand, and I don't like them!" This is a very ignorant; and sad outlook, and mentality. It is also very common, amongst our society.

Why is it so hard for us to not just change our outlook; but to practice becoming, the change? So what do people do in most cases when they fear a situation that they don't understand; and don't care to become knowledgeable about? They talk about it for the good, and the bad. We all know that words can hurt.

A large problem that many of us have with the word "truth," is not just accepting it; but the fear of living within the boundaries, of it. We fear who it will hurt, expose, how it will affect them as well as us, how it will change things; and upset, the status quo. We fear who will now look at us in a different light, question us, judge us, cut us off; or shy away from us, but why? **Why fear something that will shed light upon a dark; and confusing situation that will in turn, set us free?** When you can embrace your "truth," your mind no longer has to wonder; and you don't have to feel lost. You don't have to question the "what if's; and the why's," when you know.

So what causes an issue, or creates a problem? What creates a rift when trying to get along; and understand each other? **Is it a lie to cover up something that we did not do that we should have done; yet it will justify the circumstances as long as no one knows, but us?** Is an issue created; because we can be too prideful, and egotistic? We are unwilling to see any other way except our own; even when our way, is incorrect? Do we do this to feel as though we have the "upper hand;" until the truth, is revealed? Then we no longer have the advantage that we thought we had. Now we have a problem with our exposed reality; because it is no longer, hidden? So why not simply correct it? Why not make a wrong, a right?

Is it difficult to embrace correction; because we feel that we did nothing wrong, in the 1st place? We just did what worked for us. **We went along with our understanding according to previously learned behaviors for the good, or the bad; because it was all that we claimed to have known. Does this honestly "justify" our words, and actions?**

Everyone doesn't think, or view things the same way. For someone who has learned things an entirely different way; and went along with what worked for them despite the rifts caused, then your views may seem absurd! **This is a problem for many within our relationships; and friendships, today. We just can't seem to release the outdated mentalities that cause rifts, between these relationships. This makes it harder for us to work together.**

So how do you deal with the issues and problems that you face with your friends, boss, mate, spouse, children, family, and coworkers? **You have to break down the communication barriers; and seek to understand that effective communication, involves "give and take."** There can be no, "my way or the highway, I'm right and that's all there is to it, if you don't like it then leave, I'm the boss, this is mine, me, my, and I!" Sometimes, it's as simple as listening to another person; and seeking to understand why they feel the way, that they feel. **We all know what we are willing to tolerate. If you find yourself in a bad situation, that is about to cause serious mental, physical, and emotional harm; then let it go.**

Harboring a selfish, controlling, jealous, or possessive mentality is a terrible outlook when seeking to heal; and to move past an ongoing issue. If you are wrong and were at fault; then simply admit your error. What is so hard about admitting your own faults as an individual? Is it feeling vulnerable? Could it be, because the last time you did this; you were taken advantage of? Is it the fact that you are constantly fighting a losing battle that often ends up as a "no-win" for either party involved; because 1 of the 2 just has to have it their way, by any means necessary? This is immature behavior that can cause years of separation, resentment, bitterness, distance, emotional wear and tear, not to mention unhealthy stress that can in time lead to mental and physical breakdown.

Waging an unending battle over who is in control; and who has the upper hand is senseless, and pointless. This is often an issue within families, between siblings, amongst parents, and even friendships. Bitter enemies are created over a simple argument or disagreement; and grudges are now being held, throughout life. No one wants to be the bigger person and let go of what is no longer; or doesn't even matter anymore. We have Men and

Women who consider themselves mature adults holding onto petty issues from childhood. Why hold onto what happened 10 years ago? Was the damage caused that bad? Did someone treat you that horribly? Did they sabotage your life at that point in time? Did it affect your future goals, and interests? Did what someone say to or about you cause others to wrongfully judge; or persecute you? Did you take a vow not to rest until you make them pay; or expose them for who they really are? Why? **Is being vindictive and getting revenge so important that you allow it to poison you internally; and keep you from moving towards your desired goals, and destination in life?**

So how do we heal? When do we heal? When do we let go? Is it even possible to let go? Do we instill this ignorance, hatred, and animosity into our children? Do we tell everybody that we encounter, which in turn causes them to judge us? Healing occurs when you face the truth about a situation, or circumstance. Whether that truth hurts you, lets you down, angers, saddens, or shocks you; it will set you free internally. You will no longer have to question; or try to figure out what you needed in order to move forward with your life. This freedom in turn gives you the right to choose how you will accept and deal with your newfound knowledge. Will it destroy, and poison you internally; or will it allow you to move forward with your life, free of the chains that once had you bound, and restricted? **What do you value most: stagnation anchored by bitterness and resentment; or progression with the freedom to seek joy and peace from an ignorance that once kept you shackled, bound in pity, sadness, misery, and confusion?**

You can't change what happened to you; and you can't change the people that did the deed that was done to you, but you can change you. You can fix and correct your outlook. You can develop a more positive mentality; and move forwards. You no longer need to look back trying figure out something that you now know. Seek positive people who have overcome your challenges. Let go of; and distance yourself from those who are keeping you bound, and chained. Face your own truths. Do not hide behind them; nor blame others for faults, that are your own. This only creates bitter and resentful attitudes; especially when they, as well as you know what really happened.

It takes time and healing may not occur within a day, a week, a month, or a year. When and how you decide to heal, is determined solely by you. You know what you have to, and must do to free yourself. Seek wise counsel, and trusted advisors. Avoid negative people; and those that want to see you, continue to suffer. Just like there are good people in this world; there are bad people who thrive on the misery, chaos, and confusion of others. We all have issues, problems, difficult people, places, and circumstances to endure and face. **Do not allow a lifetime to pass, while figuring out what you need to do today in order to face, assess, and address your truth in regards to the issues that you have with others; as well as internally.** Move forward with the life you so desire. Know that you will overcome. Know that you will face your challenges, brilliantly. Know that you will not continue to suffer and feel pain, sadness, and misery. Know that you are capable of confronting your problems in a tactful and mature manner. Know that there is a positive solution. Know that you are striving to move past your pain, and towards your greater self.

Chapter 3
Life

"Will I ever get where I desire to be in life? Will I ever reach all of my goals in life; and get to a desired destination, where I can find contentment? Will I always have to struggle to find a good job; or career path, while dealing with the ups, and downs of life? When will things balance out in my life; if ever? I'm tired of using drugs, and alcohol to cope with my problems. I don't want to continue to watch my life pass me by; because I've wasted enough time, already. I need to get it together. Life is hard when you feel all alone; and have no one to turn to, for help. I can't seem to focus on my priorities; and responsibilities long enough to maintain, stability. I wish I had someone to help me. I'm tired of using excuses. Everyone I know seems to be doing better than me. Will my struggle ever end?"

Have you ever asked yourself these questions; or stated any of this? Are you still asking yourself these questions? Do you know of someone who is in a similar predicament; and that feels the same way, you do? Why, or why not?

Some people seem to just coast along through life; and it seems as if they are always granted the better, opportunities. It seems as if they are always in the right place, at the right time? As if nothing bad ever happens to them? They probably have just as many struggles; and issues as you. They also may have made better choices in determining what type of path they wanted to take for their life?

Our lives will always be sprinkled with struggle, adversity, occasional hardships, and challenges; that we must face and endure, in order to get to where we want to be in life.

Many of us have heard the saying that, "what you are supposed to be doing with your life, is probably something you have been doing your whole life?"

Now let's be realistic. The ability to find your true path can be difficult for many of us. 1 reason is; because there are endless choices, as to what you can do with your life. There are a lot of people who go into a career path at an early age; and then realize, this is not what I want to do with my life. I want to do this, I want to be here. Some people become complacent; and watch their whole lives go by thinking all the while, "should've, could've, would've." Seldom do many of us act on following through with our goals to get to our desired destination. Why? Is it because of naysayers, doubters, critics, those who pass judgment; and those who do not want to see you doing anything, that they are not?

Why is it so difficult to find our path in life; and to follow it? Does self- doubt creep in; because of failed attempts, when trying to pursue our goals? You have to make the best decisions, and choices for your life. This will ultimately, lead to your happiness. If you have a family to take care of and provide for; then pursue your personal goals and interests in your free time. Continue to maintain a sense of individuality; and work hard to get to your desired destination, in life.

Take your interests seriously. Do not just go along with something; because it seems right at the time, or it is what you need, when you need it. There will come a time when you look back to question the "why's and what ifs." Why did I do this? What if I had done that? If you find yourself at a crossroads, then understand that this isn't necessarily a bad thing. If you have established a family with let's say a wife, 2 children, a mortgage, rent, car payments, and of course bills; then it will be important to make sure that an abrupt decision to change direction, will not affect the well-being of your family.

Everyone has different ideas on what they consider being "successful." Someone may feel that as long as they are financially secure; and have accumulated more than enough money to live on they have reached the success that they measured for themselves. Someone may feel that as long as they are doing what they love; and are content with their lifestyle and choices then they have reached the success that they desire. Someone may even feel that as long as they are doing better than what they were in the past; then according to their own standards, they are "successful."

17

Finding the path that ensures that you are happy in what you are doing with your life, is your own sole vision. There are some people who judge others; and measure the success they identify with, upon "materialism." Does having an expensive luxury, sports car, a home with an awesome career, mean that you are successful? Does barely being able to pay your bills; and meet your financial obligations, although you have a vehicle that may not be in the best condition, a shabby home, and a "dead end" job, mean that you are successful? It does if you overcame conditions of poverty. You have to decide what works for you. If you envision better for yourself; then at some point, you have to stop living inside your head. Go after what you want, in a sense of "reality!"

You want to do better in terms of avoiding certain types of pitfalls, rising above obstacles, and challenges. You are not a "statistic." You want to not just feel emotionally; but to know mentally, that there can be a better way. A better way does not always mean an easier way. If you take a path that has seldom been taken; or one that the end results are unknown, then you are paving that path. You are setting the standards for what will be, and how. It is often, out of fear of the unknown; and the" what if's," that a lot of people opt to perform what has been proven to work. They see how "so in so" did it, how it worked for them; and usually imitate, that same formula.

If you choose to pave a path of your own; then you will possibly see the error in how "so in so" did it. You will possibly see how; and why it didn't work. You will also realize what could've made it work even better. You may even decide to go an entirely different route. You can have excellent results; or meet numerous obstacles and challenges, along that route.

Does this mean that you will; or have failed at what you set out to do? No. It simply means that since you are venturing into unknown territory, then results may vary. There are trial and error periods, until you reach your desired destination.

Having an optimistic state of mind is important. Seeing the glass as half empty as opposed to full can be considered as a negative outlook, one that is often deemed as "pessimistic." Whether we admit it; or not, we often become negative when things do not work out the way that we desire them to within our lives. If you seek to gain a well- paying job; and for whatever reason you lose it, then you may develop a negative outlook on "good jobs?" Most of us know someone like this; and have even felt this way about difficult circumstances, within our lives.

So why hold onto negative outlooks; and outmoded mentalities developed from failed attempts at something that wasn't right for our lives, within that moment? Is it easier to dwell upon what went wrong within our lives? It's easier to feel like the victim, as opposed to the victor. We sometimes have a tendency to enjoy pity parties. "Woe me, have mercy on me, and please feel sorry for me; because I do!" Why not change those negative circumstances? Why not correct those mistakes? Why not start over; and pave, a better way? Although we forgive the past; it's truly hard to forget the emotional strain, heartache, and hardships. We then become anchored down, by our past letdowns. We then find ourselves dwelling upon the negative. The only reason that we can't seem to get back on a better path; and start upwards once more is that, we don't allow ourselves to.

So how do we heal from our past letdowns; and get back on a better path, despite our failures? Simply assess where you went wrong, and why? Look at what you could have done differently to make a difference in the outcome of something that did not work. Take accountability for the role you played within your own situation. Could there have been a better way to say something; or to do something. Did you hold onto something past its "expiration date," while waiting for an outcome to be better? There are times when we stand in our own way; because of our reluctance to let go, change direction, or to simply stop! We are reluctant to see that what we are doing isn't working; and to start over. We fear the unknown; yet inadvertently create difficult circumstances for ourselves that in time propose a challenge to correct for ourselves. Why are we so determined to have our way that we do not realize; or overlook, "error?" You have to see the error of your own ways, in order to correct them.

Your life is your life. You have to live it to the best of your ability; regardless of what may have happened to you in the past, who may have hurt you, or let you down! It doesn't matter the terrible conditions of poverty; or dysfunction that you may have been born into. What matters is if

19

that is what you decide to dwell upon; and use as your own personal anchor to keep you firmly, rooted in place. You must be able to move forward to your desired destination in life as an adult. Break the chain!

Develop relationships with supportive and encouraging people. We all know of someone that loves dwelling upon negativity. They always brings up your past faults, and letdowns. They always ask you those same tired and worn questions about issues that no longer matter within your life. They ask you about the people, and places that kept you down. "Does he still do this? Does she still treat you like that? Are they still giving you a hard time? Do you still feel the same way? Remember this, remember that? Are you still doing the same thing?"

Negative people ask you all of those horrible questions that send your mind traveling backwards and dwelling upon what no longer serves a purpose within your life. You are not only trying to move on, but to become better! Why do they ask you those silly and ridiculous questions? Release yourself and get away from these types of people.

An unfortunate reality for some, is that most of the people that we know who keep us down just so happens to consist of our family, and close friends? Why? These are the people that are supposed to help us. They should want to see us doing well; and pursuing the objectives that make us happy, right? Some of them do not want to see you doing better than them. Some of them have yet to figure out; or even attempt to heal from the hurt and pain, that they harbor inside. **Naturally, they just don't know how to help you; because they have yet to help themselves**. Is this a bad thing? No. it means that you are not the only one enduring what you view as "your struggle," so don't feel alone.

Oftentimes, it is hard to find someone to trust, and confide in. It can be difficult finding someone who shares our goals, supports our dreams, and nurtures our visions. Most of us are hesitant to share our personal affairs and private matters with total strangers. We fear judgment, gossip, and ridicule. We fear the negativity that will surround our choices, and decisions. We fear the judgmental views and opinions of others. Where do we find supportive people who are going through similar changes? Where do we find the people that not only feel similar to the way that we feel; but that are in need of healing, as well?

Where do we find these trustworthy and supportive people? Are they in the Church? Can they be found amongst co-workers, upon our jobs? Are they the people that we have known for a lifetime, and grew up with? Are they the parents, friends, relatives, counselors, mentors, teachers, advocates, or prestigious people within our communities? There are people who exist that you can confide in that are willing to not only listen to what you are saying; but seek to understand why, and to help you achieve your aims. There are people who exist that are willing to give you sound and valuable advice; whether it is to your liking, or not. It doesn't matter whether you agree or not. They are always there to assist you. They are genuine. These are the types of people that are great to surround yourself with. It is important to have supportive people that are willing to offer a hand of encouragement, help, guidance, and correction.

Whether they are there for a season; or a lifetime, may not be within our control. Whether or not the knowledge, help, support, and friendship can be temporary; or lasting, is up to us to decide.

Some of us need more help than others; because we have been through so much. If you are still standing today at this moment; regardless of how hard your life may have been, then know that you are here for a purpose, and for a reason. So many people today get where they desire to be in life; and choose not to look or reach back to help someone else, along the way. So many people today get where they desire to be; and pretend as if they never had to endure a struggle, hard times, and could care less about the next man, or woman's adversities.

Finding, and setting along the right life path will not always be an easy task. There will be temptations, pitfalls, hurdles, challenges, obstacles, sufferings, and hardships. Mistakes can be what lead us to failure, and ruin. Mistakes can also be utilized as valuable lessons that can push you forward, when you feel like stopping; and giving up. Seek to move ahead with the knowledge of what yesterday's past taught you. Allow these present lessons to pave the way for a better and brighter future. **Do not walk in the fear of**

failure. Walk in the knowledge of what you have learned; and know that you are capable of winning.

Face, assess, and address your truths in regards to where you are in life. Be willing to seek the healing within your truth; in order to move forward, with your life. You can, and will have the life that you desire. You can be happy. You can find peace. You can overcome the adversities that you face. You will overcome the challenges that seem, too difficult. You are not a failure nor a loser; but a winner. You will continue to endure struggles, at some point in time. You will continue to strive toward your desired destination in life. You will not give up. Continue to believe in you, the dreams and goals that you have set; as well as your ability to attain them.

Chapter 4
Career

"I don't know why I continue to wake up; and go to this same old mundane, job. This is not what I want to be doing with my life. I do not feel a sense of fulfillment from these tasks. This job just doesn't pay enough money for me to live; and provide for my family. I never saw the day that I would get stuck making a living doing such a job. There has to be something better! I need to be doing what I always envisioned myself doing for a living. I need to become my own boss. This place is just not for me! I feel like I am robbing myself of my true potential. There has to be a better way. There has to be something better out there for me that is fulfilling! I'm not happy with where I am currently in life, with this job. I'm tired of struggling to pay the bills; and to make ends meet!"

Have you ever woke up and found yourself pondering such thoughts to; and from your way, to work? Has someone questioned you recently as to why you do what you do for a living; and the purpose you feel that it serves, within your life? Does it not only pay the bills; but does it fulfill you? Are you working the job that you always dreamed about? Well, if you're like most people, then you are probably working to pay the bills; and to pay off debts. In the back of your mind, you know that place that you call a job, just isn't for you! So why are you still there? Are you stuck?

So when do you decide to make that move towards what you want to be doing with your life in terms of a job; or a career? Is it too late? Are you fully invested, and waiting until you can retire? Will you be there for x amount of more years; because that just seems to be all there is for, your life?

When will you wake up; and start living your dream, and walking in the purpose that you envision for yourself? We often take on a job as adults then purchase vehicles, apartments, homes, marry, date, have children; and take on debts that we have to pay for. Depending upon what we are doing on a job; and how much it pays, we base our standards of living around it. We put personal fulfillment within the back of our minds; yet time continues to pass, on by. We eventually realize that we are selling ourselves short. We are robbing ourselves of our own personal inner joy from doing what we truly enjoy.

Is it ever too late to start over; and to start pursuing our dream job, or career path? Of course not. There are people of different ages, and backgrounds going back to school to pursue their passion. Look at all of the self-made millionaires, gurus, entertainers, artists, celebrities, and common people who 1 day decided to wake up; and pursue their dream, in spite of. Anything worth having is worth working towards. Does this mean that the odds of you becoming who you always envisioned yourself being are slim to none? No. **Your drive, ambition, and willpower to get to your desired destination in life are the determining factors.** Let's look at a few scenarios:

Scenario 1- (Behind closed doors, a young man struggles throughout his life to find his own individual career path. He is good at almost anything he sets his mind to accomplish; yet he has a hard time focusing upon 1 task, and completing it to fruition. He endures years of hardship; and struggles, financially. He enjoys computers, and technology. He has a keen intellect; and is very good at solving riddles, and decoding numbers. He 1 day creates an application to make organization, and structure easier for those who have the same trouble that he has, in terms of focusing. He seeks to share his idea with a well-known celebrity. The celebrity steals his idea, and makes it his own; because he has the money, power, and resources to do so. The young man can't afford a lawyer; and is unable to fight to rightfully claim, what is his. He does not become discouraged. Time continues to pass; and he once again creates an entirely different application to share, and help others. This time, instead of seeking the help of a well-known person; he takes it upon himself to get his idea and name, on the market. He continues to struggle and endure financially; and then 1day awakens to the realization that he has become a millionaire! He is sought by many for his unique; and intelligent perspective in solving, and dealing with everyday problems and issues, through the utilization of modern technology. **Does this ever occur today in real life? Is it possible to endure challenges; and adversities to find your path, yet through diligence, and perseverance to 1 day wake up where you always dreamed that you would be? What are the odds of this happening? Is it wise to share your ideas when you need help; or lack the resources and connections, to get your idea out there? Are there people who will take advantage of you and steal your ideas, in order to benefit from them? What is something that this young man could have changed about his outlook to better his predicament; and to prevent his financial struggles?**)

Scenario 2-(Behind closed doors, a single mother works a mundane; and mediocre job that pays little to provide a life for her, and her child. In her mind, she envisions herself going back to school; and finding a profession that she will be able to enjoy, to provide a better lifestyle. She struggles to get the assistance to get into college. Her peers; and close ones attended, but did not finish. They are reluctant to help her. Although she doesn't make much money; she is told that she makes too much to qualify for financial aid. Since she does not have knowledgeable people within her life; she continues to work her mediocre job until 1 day on that job, she talks with a co-worker who is about to graduate from college. She instructs her on how to get into school; and helps her, with the application process. She eventually does further her education; and attains a career within a sought after field, making 3 times what she had been accustomed to. She is content with where she now is in life; and chooses not to pursue further ambitious endeavors. The woman becomes a mentor; and a role model to single mothers who want to better their lives, but don't know how to. **Is this possible? Can people today struggle to survive; and lack the knowledge to pursue their dreams, and goals? Can we meet other people who are willing to help, and guide us toward our goals? Is it possible to better your position in life; regardless of what your personal situation may be? Can this woman be considered a role model within her community, and amongst society? Is this woman justified for not wanting more out of life, although she is capable of achieving more? How important is it to seek balance; and to find contentment, as well as fulfillment in life?**)

Scenario 3- (Behind closed doors, a middle-aged couple struggle to provide for; and raise their children. They work but do not make much money, yet they have love. They work well as a team, and share similar visions for their future. The couple desires to create a program that will encourage; and inspire others within their predicament. They endure years of strife; and 1 day the man, loses his job. The woman continues to support the family, while the man begins to research how to make their dream goal attainable; and bring it into fruition. After several years of letdown, and rejection; they decide to invest the little money they have saved into their program, in order to get it off the ground. Within a year, the program becomes duplicated by investors who see the potential within it. This creates millionaires out of a couple who once struggled to maintain; and who lived paycheck, to paycheck. **Is this possible? Is it ever too late to pursue long sought after goals, and dreams in spite of age; or how much time it takes, to reach them? Do we see this everyday somehow, somewhere, and in some form? Why do we have so many people who give up on their dreams; and goals before they can ever achieve them? them? Is it important to see ordinary people accomplishing great feats in life; regardless of their economic condition? Do we sometimes hinder our own progress by judging ourselves; or others too harshly? Is it ever a good idea not to dream big; or envision ourselves in a better predicament? How did not giving up affect the outcome of their dreams?**)

The fact that you have bills should not keep you from pursuing your ideal career path. Bills and debts have been around for a very long time; and will continue to exist as long as money, and the need for services provided exist. An important factor to consider is- will you be able to maintain your financial obligations while pursuing your chosen career path? If you have a mortgage, kids in college, car notes, and a sick mother in the nursing home that you are having to provide for financially; then of course, you can't just quit your day job to pursue your dream job. However, you may can get into college; and take some classes online, within your free time. If you are on child support for 3 children, and paying alimony; then you can't just quit your day job. However; you can pursue further education, as well as your ideal job as a hobby. Who knows what this hobby will produce in time if you take it seriously, and continue to persevere? If you consider yourself alone and have only you to take care of; then why not pursue your ambitions? Why not set meaningful and attainable goals for you to reach? Why are you working a mediocre job that pays little to nothing; when you desire to have so much more for yourself? Why struggle, when you honestly don't have to?

What keeps us from pursuing our desired career path in life? Is it because we lack the knowledge to get there; and are reluctant to ask questions? Do we feel as though we do not have supportive people within our lives? Do we feel as though it is senseless to take a chance on an idea, when we have a concrete job opportunity at our disposal; although it may not benefit us in the long term? What is the problem? What are we afraid of? Are we afraid to fail? Do we fear rejection, when we can maintain the comfort within complacency?

The only thing that is standing in your way is you! Although you may have experienced letdown the last time that you attempted to pursue your passion; this does not mean that it isn't for you. **A failed attempt should be considered a lesson; and what do we do with lessons? We learn from them**. Question, and assess why something did not work out for you. What could you have done differently? What would have made things easier for you? Many people say that if only they knew then what they know now; then things would be different. So now that you know what you know; why are things still the same? When will the change within your life for the better occur? When will you decide to go after what you want in a sensible manner, without jeopardizing what you have already established? This is possible. It will take careful and considerate planning; especially when you have other financial obligations, and responsibilities to fulfill.

Change not only occurs within; but it starts with you. You decide, and determine the outcome to your situation. You know if that job that you get up and go to work for 12 hours at a time, isn't for you; when you're only bringing home 6 hours -worth of pay? You know that you are smarter, and capable of doing more than washing a vehicle for a living. Do not rob yourself of your greater potential. You know that you are capable of greater accomplishments in life; when you graduated #1 in your high school class. You know that no matter who tells you how dumb; or stupid you are for making the mistakes that you have made, that you are intelligent. You can, and will overcome all of the negative obstacles within your life. You know that even though you come from a family that just settled for what life has to offer; that you can break the cycle, and go after what you want. You are greater than your circumstances, and can do better! **You decide!**

If you need help with determining your career path; and what will aid you in getting to the next level, then do not hesitate to seek wise counsel, as well as trusted advisors. Do not share a million dollar vision, with a person who is content with living paycheck to paycheck. They will not understand your vision! Do not be satisfied with nothing when you continue to know within the back of your mind, that you deserve something. Figure out what you enjoy doing and seek to turn it into a career path. Do not be afraid to assess where you are in terms of work; and if you are not happy then stop continuing to settle. Go after what you want; and don't just "feel" like it's for you, but "know" that it is for you!

Be willing to network with positive people who want to see you succeed; and that are unselfish enough to help you reach, and attain your goals. Speak positivity in your own life; and don't just talk about it, but be about it. Take action. Map out, plan your goals, and mark them off as you reach them. Continue to set attainable goals, until you reach them all. Develop an ambitious attitude; and strive towards, the will to succeed! You should not 1 day wake up thinking that you should've, could've, would've; but instead wake up thinking, "I did, and I'm glad I did it." I am happy with where I am in life. **You realize fulfillment when you enjoy what you do; and you don't have to question why you do it.**

Healing from past letdowns; and failures is different for us all in regards to, career path. Some people fall down; and never find their way back up, because they give up on themselves. Some people get up; and never look back down, because they no longer need to be reminded where they came from. They become focused on staying where they worked so hard to get to. This is not a crime. It's their choice. As opposed to worrying about why someone is where they are, how they got there, criticizing, and judging;

do not hesitate to learn from their experiences. You may be aided through their example, in how to get where you desire to be.

Be willing to face, assess, and address your truth, in regards to why you are not where you desire to be in terms of career. Seek to find the healing within these truths; so that you may set yourself along, a better path. Learn from your mistakes; and view them as lessons, so that you may correct your errors. Strive to reach the success that you desire for your own life. Set reachable and attainable goals. Do not only live inside your head; but desire to take action, in reality. Act upon the thoughts, ideas, and the dreams that you have for yourself. Make positive changes for the better, within your life. Know that you will find a career that is great for you; and that meets your needs. Do not let negativity become the chains that anchor you to a place, you do not see fit for yourself. Maintain a positive outlook. Surround yourself with positive; and supportive people, who will encourage you. Know that you can have the career that you desire. Know that you are not stuck in a position that is of no benefit to you or your family. Know that you can start over. Do not be afraid to ask for help. Do not fear rejection. Be willing to let go of negative thoughts. Embrace the power of positive thinking as you move towards your greater self.

Chapter 5
Finances

"I'm sick and tired of living paycheck to paycheck, week to week, month to month, year in, and year out! The money I make just isn't enough to provide for me, and my family. I just had my car repossessed; and now I'm getting evicted from my apartment. I can't afford to pay child support and continue to live; because I just don't make enough money. I need a new car; but I can't afford another monthly bill right now. If only I had more money! I can't afford to take my family on a vacation this year, since I lost my job. I can't pay all these bills at once; so I guess I will have to decide if the light or the gas bill is more important? I go to work every day; but since I don't make much, my paycheck does not amount to anything. I took on a 2nd job just to take care of my family; but it still isn't enough. I went through all my savings, when I was unemployed."

Have you found yourself stating any of this as of late? Do you know someone going through and enduring similar hardships? Why is it so hard for some of us to find the jobs making the money that we need to survive? Why do we have to struggle financially far too often in life?

Sound familiar? Despite what you may have heard; if you haven't realized it by now, money really does matter. How important is having a well-paying job or career to you? How important is it to be able to comfortably provide and take care of your family, for you? Do we as people in today's society put too much emphasis on money; or perhaps not enough? **Are we educating our children to properly and responsibly handle and maintain their finances?**

Why is money and finances so important? You honestly can't lead a normal, healthy, and productive lifestyle maintaining your bills; as well as your responsibilities without it. **When you add rent, mortgages, household expenses, vehicles, gas, maintenance, debts, clothing, groceries, childcare expenses, and needs to the equation; if you don't make enough money you will run into some serious hurdles and challenges!**

1 of the most important things that we can do in regards to our "finances," is to get educated. Do not settle for less when you know that you deserve more. Do not seek a job just to say that you are working and maintaining. Seek a "career" in which you can prosper and find fulfillment. Research and find out about your chosen field of study and what it pays short term and long term.

Do not settle for less. College is not for everyone and everyone does not, and will not attend. If you decide to work a "job," make sure that it is a well-paying job. Make sure that you can provide for yourself as well as your family and other needs with the pay from that job. Make sure that there is "advancement" upon that job if you do so choose to stay on it. Seek to climb the ladder of success and set goals and have ambitions. If you work a job in which you can go back to school or attain certifications in order to make more money, as well as become a specialist in that field; then do so! **Do not waste your time or energy simply falling into a monotonous and "dead end" routine, with no hope or desire to earn more.**

Seek a job that does give promotions and has excellent benefits. Time is something that you can't get back and when it's gone it's gone. No one wants to look back and see that nothing was ever attained, gained, nor achieved through years of their hard work. Make enough money in which you have at least something left to save after each paycheck, if possible. **Many people believe that you should save something if only a little; yet if you make only a little then there's nothing left to save, because nothing from nothing leaves nothing.** Strive to make something to put away for a rainy day; because the day will come, and who knows how long the rain will last?

Value your self- worth. Do not settle for just anything, because everything isn't good for you. We often realize this a day late, and more than a dollar short. Derive a budget and do not just fit your expenditures within this budget; but your earnings as well. If you pay out more than what you are bringing in; then this only results in debt, because you are left within the negative. So always make sure you can afford the lifestyle you feel that you deserve. Working 2 or 3 jobs is impressive yet; why work 2 or 3 when you can find 1 that is equivalent in pay to those extra 2? Working numerous jobs; often takes away from the time you should invest within your family and personal life. This in turn leads to a neglected family, unhealthy relationships, and a sad personal life.

Avoid becoming a lender nor a borrower if at all possible, because you are not a bank. If you don't make enough money to begin with; then you probably won't make enough money to pay back, so avoid this. In most cases; borrowing money becomes a bottomless pit; because with interests and unseen expenditures that will crop up you will be left within the negative. Avoid working hard just to neglect paying the bills that matter; because your focal point has changed to the 1 that could have been avoided. This will result in a poor credit rating either way you look at it in the long run; because something is going to have to go unpaid. A pie can only be divided so many ways; and everyone you owe a slice, will always want their piece.

Live within your means. We all desire a fine lifestyle and to live above average; yet the question is, "can you afford to do so?" Struggling to stay afloat is seldom impressive especially when you could have gone with what you could have afforded in the meantime; until you got to where you desired to be in time. Strive to set reachable goals to attain the type of lifestyle that you feel that you deserve. If you make $8.00 an hour; you can't live on an $18.00 an hour budget. The only thing you will increase is your debts; quick, fast, and in a hurry which often results in loss at some point in time. Loss in the form of foreclosures, evictions, repossessions, and bankruptcies are indeed common! These losses rarely and seldom discriminate, when the due date is past date.

Avoid becoming complacent. It's easy to become comfortable and stagnant when we feel everything is going as well as it can. Ask yourself, "Can it possibly be better?" If so, then how? What will it take to earn more, to pay off debts, and to get ahead, as opposed to behind? It may take a whole other job, harder work, or a total change in career and vocation? **Do not be afraid to make a change that will better your life, financially.** Do not assume and anticipate the worst will happen if you decide to make a better choice and decision in order to do and be better; as well as to attain more. There are times when we have to evaluate our situation and take healthy and well-calculated risks. There are times when we have to step outside of our comfort zone in order to embrace something that we may have missed unintentionally, and unknowingly.

Sometimes, it's not just about vocation; but location. If you live in an area where there isn't much employment opportunity catering to your specific skillset; then you may want to consider moving to an area or location where jobs within your skillset are available. In most cases; certain areas, cities, and states will pay a whole other amount that can be greater than what you are currently earning; because your specific skill set may be in demand? Often, our families, children, and friends will keep us rooted in a certain environment in which we call "home." If you are content with the status quo, then by all means; maintain your peace and happiness. However, if you desire to do better and attain more; and you have no fears nor commitments when it comes to changing your environment and moving towards progress, then do so!

Let's take a look at a couple of scenarios:

Scenario1-(Behind closed doors; a young woman is preparing to graduate from college. She has diligently and dutifully worked a part-time job making mediocre pay throughout college to provide for herself. She has a mother and 2 younger siblings that she helps whenever possible financially. Her father is active in her life; but he doesn't live within the home and he and the mother are divorced. The mother works a job and does not make a lot of money and so she struggles to take care of and provide for her household. The mother is prideful and does not ask for help or assistance from her relatives or the government. Although she would like to attain a better job to improve her circumstances; she lacks the drive, will, and determination to do so. She does not mind asking her daughter for help. Upon graduating from college; the young daughter is preparing to enter into a branch of the military. The mother pleads her not to go and tells her that she needs to stay close to home to help her and her siblings. She emotionally manipulates the young woman. The young woman decides to pursue a job within her career field that is close to home. Although she has a college degree; the wages from the jobs within her community are not competitive. The young woman will have to settle for making a little more than she did working part-time through college. The difference is that she will now have excellent benefits on her job as a full-time employee. The young woman, in time becomes resentful toward her mother for intervening in her future plans for her life. The mother is content; because she can continue to depend upon her adult daughter for help with providing and maintaining her household. **Does this happen amongst our society today? Is the mother of the college graduate wrong for "using" her daughter as a crutch? Is the daughter at fault for helping her mother and her siblings? Would you put your life on hold to stay behind to help your family financially? Why or why not? What needs to occur in order for**

the mother to heal from her past faults and letdowns and to become independent? Why do you think the mother depends upon her daughter for help, instead of striving to do better for herself? How will the mother's behavior influence the outlook of the 2 younger siblings?)

Scenario 2-(A young man suffers financially behind closed doors. He is a hard worker, but he takes mediocre jobs, and feels that is better than not working at all. The jobs he works only pay a little above minimum wage. The young man is single and considers himself as being independent; yet he struggles to provide for himself because he doesn't make enough money. He drives an old worn vehicle that needs constant work, he lives in a shabby apartment, and he struggles to pay his rent as well as to keep his utilities on. His friends and relatives constantly encourage him to pursue a better job; but he is content and does not desire anything greater from life, financially. As the young man gets older; he realizes that his peers are moving onward with their lives and pursue better opportunities and avenues to provide for their families. The young man decides to seek better employment; but has a hard time finding a better job because he only has a specific skillset, that is only catered to on the job that he has worked for years. The young man debates whether or not to go back to school; but he doesn't know how he will continue to pay his bills and pursue an education simultaneously? The young man feels stuck and becomes confused as to which avenue to take in order to better his financial circumstances. His peers continue to move forward with their lives as he continues to waste valuable time; pursuing a "dead end" job. **Does this happen amongst our society today? Why do you think it is hard for the young man to move forward with his life, financially? Is it possible to become "stuck" in predicaments such as this 1? How? Is the young man wasting time by continuing to work the "dead end" job and not pursuing a college education? What does this young man need to do in order to heal from his past mistakes, and to move forward in a positive and productive direction with his life and career? Could a mentor, guide, or role model make a difference in the mentality and outlook of this young man; in regards to life and the importance of financial education?)**

When it comes to Healing in regards to your finances; always remember that it is never too late to start over and get your financial house in order. The mistakes that we make with money in our early 20's will be totally different by the time you reach your early 30's; because countless lessons should have been learned within that time frame in terms of the do's and don'ts. We should realize what has, can, and will hurt us, financially. If you grew up struggling and watching your parents and family not having enough money; we often say, "That will never be me!" Then once we do get in a position to earn a little money, what happens? It often runs through our fingers like water! Why? It happens because now we are in a position where we don't have to go without! If you want it and can afford it; then you can have it! Now we have created a new habit of buying what we want and more so than not; something occurs that puts us in a financial strain and bind? The car needs maintenance, the past due bill suddenly becomes due with late fees attached! Now we are in a position to where we may have to "rob Peter to pay Paul," because although we had the money, we spent it! So not only have we created a bad habit that is about to possibly get worse before it gets better; we have hurt ourselves, financially.

The best thing to do; is not to do. A bad habit is usually formed when we do something we should have never done in the 1st place? We see the negative end results it has on those around us and we think to ourselves, "It will never be me!" In time, it ends up being exactly you! If we already know what is not good for us; then we must learn to practice self-discipline. Learn to avoid digging holes for ourselves that become deeper and harder to get out of, when we continue to make the same mistakes time and time again.

When in a process of healing financially; we must not be afraid to ask for help. We are often ashamed to state how much debt we have personally. It is embarrassing for your friends and loved ones to know that you are struggling just to keep a roof over your head, provide food and shelter for your children, pay the bills on time, and to keep from getting evicted and losing it all. It hurts to have to ask to borrow money not just once; but on a seemingly regular basis, because there is hardly ever anything left once you cash your paycheck. It never seems to be enough. So why not ask for help? **Why continue borrowing money that you can't pay back when you can just simply assess your situation and ask for the specific type of help you need? Consult a financial advisor, debt relief counselor, an accountant?**

A problem that we often do not see as an issue until it's too late is working a dead end job; a job with no form of advancement, no climbing up the ladder of success, no raises or promotions, and a poor pay scale. When trying to live like a king or queen on a peasant pay scale; you will either make numerous sacrifices, often going without what you desire to have; or accumulate some serious debt. So if you envision yourself living a grand and luxurious, or simply comfortable lifestyle; then figure out what it will take to get there, and how to maintain it once you gain it.

Many jobs today use temporary companies who work as middlemen to find the unemployed jobs. How does this work? You apply for a job through the temporary agency. The agency sets you up for an interview with an employer. The employer may hire you paying you only a percentage of your hourly pay while the other percentage goes to the temporary agency for locating you the job. You sign a contract to work under the temporary agency; although you go to the actual employer's place of business to perform your duties. You may be considered temporary for 90 days, 6 months, a year, or longer! In numerous cases, you have no insurance, no 401k, no vacation days or sick time accumulated and no holiday pay during this "trial period." No benefits. The employer can terminate your assignment whenever they desire to do so for whatever reason; and then you are left to start all over again. Many people are currently working through a temporary agency all the while hoping, Praying, and wishing that they will eventually gain a full-time job with benefits. Numerous employers are continuing to save money, while the temporary agencies make money off of you.

This can hurt you financially; because if you gain a temporary assignment making fairly decent money for x amount of time, and then base your standard of living off of this temporary assignment? You will lose in more ways than 1, when the assignment ends. There are cases in which after x amount of time working a job through a temporary agency; that an employee does get hired on permanently through a company. This can, and does happen as well.

Do not hesitate to map out your desired destination. If you find yourself within a negative predicament financially; write down a plan assessing, and addressing how you got into that negative predicament. Write down the necessary steps to take in order to get out of that predicament. Stick to the script! We often know how to solve our own problems; we just have a problem making the necessary adjustments that it will take to do so. Confide in a trusted friend for advice. Someone that you know wants to see you succeed and that will motivate you and encourage you to stay on track. Allow them to "help" you. Focus on breaking the bad habits created that allowed you to fall in the 1st place. Realize that you will not allow this to occur anymore, once you are victorious in climbing out of this hole!

Everyone makes mistakes, and some of our greatest mistakes can be the best lessons that we ever learned. Do not be afraid to learn from yourself. Figure out why you did not succeed and avoid that step on the next go around. Do not fear failure. Think positively and do not be weighed down by negativity. Do not confide in those whom will gossip and ridicule you. Negativity will cloud your judgment and hinder your progress, as well as growth. Do what it takes to better your situation.

Healing takes time and will be a tedious process. Do not fear the time that it takes for you to grow and correct your wrongs, financially. Know that you will overcome. Know that you are not the only person to ever be where you are financially; and you will never be the last.

Avoid continuing to engage in the same harmful and toxic spending patterns and habits. Once you learn from your mistake; seek to not do the same thing once more. Break the cycle! Have faith in yourself and think positively. Ask for help. There is always available help and resources. You will overcome. You will endure. You can gain control of your financial situation and turn it from a negative to a positive. You are capable of having what you desire, being where you envision yourself, and no longer suffering from financial burdens! You will grow into a more prosperous and productive individual. You can and will do better in regards to your finances. **Do not be afraid to, face, assess, and address the truth in regards to your financial situation, in order to embrace the healing within. Prepare to embrace your better and greater self.**

Chapter 6
Family

"I wish that I could get along better with the members of my family. I don't really know my family; because they were not present, nor involved within my life. I'm better off not knowing or dealing with my family. This family has issues. I don't deal with my relatives. I don't associate with the members of my immediate family; because they have too many issues and problems. I didn't want my family so I went out and created a family that I did want. I love my family in spite of. I have a wonderful family. I am thankful to have such amazing people to call, "family."

Have you ever found yourself stating, or feeling any of this? Do you know of anyone else that feels the same way about their family; or view them within a similar light? Why do you or others think, and feel this way about your family?

"Family," is a word that has numerous meanings depending upon who you ask. What does family mean to you? Do you have a great family that gets along well? Do you come from a dysfunctional family? Are your relatives family-oriented? Does your family embrace; and accept each other lovingly? Is there resentment, anger, or bitterness amongst your family members? Is there a reason; or something beyond your control, that is straining your relationship with your "family?"

Why does it have to be so difficult for many of our families amongst society, to get along with each other? Why do some of us tend to lead our lives living within the boundaries of a lie; or an assumption created to justify and to limit our potential, in terms of growing and moving forward emotionally, as a family? We all make mistakes as well as do and say things that we are not proud of. People have the freedom, as well as the right to be who they desire to be. We know and are aware of this. Yet

my question is; why does this notion have such a damaging effect upon our "families?" Let's look at a few scenarios:

Scenario 1-(Behind closed doors, a young man and woman establish a relationship. They date and have fun, as well as 2 children. They do not marry. Eventually time and circumstance takes a toll for the worse upon the relationship. The man and woman decide to separate; leaving the woman to raise the children as a single mother. The man moves away to another state and eventually marries, builds a life, and a family to call his own. The mother chooses not to ask the man for financial help for the children. She is resentful and harbors anger towards him for leaving them behind; and moving on with his life. She is reluctant to move on with her own life; and lives through her children. When they ask about their father, she tells them that he does not care about them. She assures them that they can depend on her for all of their needs and wants. The children grow older and although the father calls often to talk to them; the mother does not inform them, for she is still bitter. The children grow into adults. 1 child seeks to find the father to establish a relationship with him. The father embraces her. He wants her and her sibling to know that he loved them always; and considers them his family, regardless. The other child can't stand the father, and does not want to have anything to do with him. The father is hurt and saddened by this. The mother feels no remorse for what she instilled within the children. She has yet to face her truth, and to heal. **Does this occur within our society today? Is the angry child wrong for harboring resentment towards the father? Was the father wrong for moving on with his life? Is the child who reached out to the father justified? Do we have mothers within our society that harbor bitterness and resentment towards fathers today? How can this family of people heal and embrace their truth within this situation? Is it even possible?**)

Scenario2- (Behind closed doors, a man enjoys life to the full. He enjoys engaging in intimate encounters with random women. He creates numerous children through these encounters; all by different mothers. The man is not interested in settling down; and leads a selfish life revolving around him doing as he pleases, when he pleases. The women reach out to the man for financial support to aid the children; yet he evasively avoids them. He seems to get off the hook "scotch free" until he gets older; and has a reversal of fortune in health, and finance. The children grow into adults. The father is now sickly with no place to go. He reaches out to the children that he denied, for help and support. Out of 6 children, 2 embrace the man. They have forgiven him; and accept the truth within the situation. The other 4 talk negatively to and about the man, and ridicule him. 1 of the 4 even threatens the father's life if he continues to reach out to him. The father seeks forgiveness; and is saddened, for he now lives a life of regret and sorrow. **Are the 4 children who harbor resentment and anger toward the man justified? Did the 2 who reached out to embrace the father; although he wasn't there for them, do the "right" thing? What could the father have done differently to prevent the situation he created for himself, in having children which do not think much of him? Is it possible for everyone to face, address, and assess the truth regarding this situation, in order to heal?)**

Scenario3- (Behind closed doors, a family consisting of a mother, father, and 3 children endure hardships and struggles to provide; and make it in today's society, as a family. They do not have much; but they have love. The father works a difficult job that does not pay much; while the mother works odd and end jobs to help provide food for the table, utilities, and a roof over their heads. They do not make much because they do not have college educations. The father was a high school dropout; and the mother only has a GED. They do not pursue their education; because they are busy trying to provide for, and raise their family. They are seldom home due to work; yet they instill great morals, values, and teachings within their children. They have love. When the 3 children grow up and enter into adulthood; 1 becomes a doctor, 1 becomes a lawyer, and 1 is a cashier at a grocery store. The doctor and the lawyer look down upon their family; and have disowned them. They do not call, visit, nor do they seem to care. They feel as though their parents were wrong for seldom being present, when they were growing up. They only associate with those they consider on their "level;" and look down upon their family. They tell lies to their friends; and have created false depictions as to where, and how they actually grew up. The 1 child who is a cashier, is very close to her parents.

She reaches out to her siblings; yet they avoid and ignore her. They feel as though they are too good for their own family. **How often does this happen amongst society today? Is it common; and can it be classified as normal behavior? Why do the 2 successful children feel as though they have to be ashamed of the truth about their identity; and where they come from? Is the child that is a cashier wrong for continuing to embrace her family; and reaching out to the ones who have disowned her? Is it possible for this family to face, assess, and address, their truth in order to heal within this situation?**)

Why do we have people that are ashamed of their backgrounds; and where they come from amongst today's society? Are we ever justified for looking down upon our own families, and the members that may not be doing as good as we are; or as we think they should be? Are we honestly doing as well as we think that we are, in all actuality? Can we blame our upbringing and conditioning as being the reasons to why we feel the way some of us tend to?

When it comes to our past pains, faults, and letdowns in terms of our families; how and when do we heal? Why do we have so many fathers abandoning our mothers and children within our society today? Are these men simply moving on from a bad relationship or situation? Why are they not taking care of the children created through those relationships? Why do we have so many hurt children that are growing into angry, bitter, and resentful adults? Is it because they are unaware of the "truth" as to what really occurred; or do they even care to know? **Why are there so many mothers that have to take on the role of single parent?** Why are our mothers speaking negatively and harshly to the children, about their fathers? Why are so many women harboring so much anger and resentment towards these men; that they use the children as tools of leverage, to control and manipulate the man's thoughts, feelings, and actions? Is any of this bizarre behavior justified? When and how do we heal?

Healing does and will occur when you decide to face, assess, and address your truth in a mature and tactful manner. We all know that there are some "truths" that we are unwilling to deal and cope with; because they are too hurtful and painful. We have family secrets that are destroying families. We have men that choose not claim, nor embrace their children. There are men who are not mature enough to take responsibility and accountability for themselves; nor are they stable enough financially, mentally, or emotionally. These same men are aiding in the creation of lives, for others to take care of. We have men simply not being men.

We have women within our society today that have yet to live their lives, enjoy the things that they want to do and experience for themselves; yet they are falling in love with men who are selling them the dream that they will help them to attain these certain types of lifestyles and provide for them. When children become involved; they become a totally different person? **Lies are being told, people are being deceived, children are being robbed, and we are inadvertently creating cycles for ourselves as well as our families; that are becoming harder, and harder to break.** The negative cycles are becoming a part of our realities. These cycles are being considered normal and typical behavior for better; or for worse. This is making it harder and harder to move past our past, as well as to figure out how to let go and start over; because these are actual changes that are occurring within our lives! All this negativity that we see, hear, read, and talk about is not just becoming common; but it's real.

You have to determine and figure out if the person you are deciding to date, marry, and have children with is right for you. You have to decide if they are stable enough and goal-oriented for you. You have to decide if there is something wrong with them mentally, emotionally, or physically; and whether or not you can help them. You have to know when it is ok to let go. It shouldn't be 2-3 kids later; and you've tried everything possible just to make it work. By this time; you may have become bitter, resentful, or angry. You have to decide when to be honest with yourself, your partner, as well as these children as to what you can; or can't do, and why.

You have to decide to step up and better your life not just for you when there are children involved; because what you do will affect the outlook of your children and possibly their actions. You set the example.

If you are unprepared to create, raise, provide for, and to take care of a family; then stop deceiving others just for a moment of intimacy, when you already know the truth. If a person doesn't meet your standards; then stop pretending as though you are giving them a chance. When things don't work out the way you plan; you allow that instance to become what you consider, to be your greatest mistake in life. You knew all along that it wasn't right. People know when they are trying to take advantage of a person or a situation; so why get upset, run, hide, and lie when the consequences arise? We have to learn to think, before we act. Our actions are not only causing problems for the lives of our families; but for these innocent children who don't ask to be here. The children are having to suffer; because you don't have it together, and have yet to figure it out.

We must take accountability and responsibility for our actions, faults, and misdeeds. We must not be afraid to face our "truths;" because this is when our healing will begin. It will be difficult at times. It may hurt. It may cause upsets. When you become involved in someone else's life and create a life; it's not just about you anymore. You have now involved others. You are now affecting the health, well-being, and the outcome of someone else's life.

We have too many broken families; and too many hurt children, that are not at fault for the adult's decisions and choices. We have too many mothers raising these children alone; and there are too many men claiming that the child is not theirs, all the while creating more children to deny. We have to face, assess, and address our truth for better; or for worse, in order to heal. When we act without thinking; or when things turn out in ways we did not plan for them to, reality is still reality. Accountability and responsibility is a must if we are ever going to change things for the better, in terms of family. A child shouldn't have to grow up and envision a tree with no leaves, when they think of the word family. They should see a strong and mighty tree that is full of beautiful and healthy leaves, that stands radiant amongst the sun!

We do not choose and can't help who our family members are. Some of us have drug addicts, alcoholics, mental illness, criminals; and a host of other negative circumstances, that we can't control within our families. Many of us are the products of these circumstances; and that's why we feel the way

43

we feel. This does not mean that you have to disown your family. Why not reach out to help them? If you can't help them; then why not try to get them some help? Why do we have to act as if we don't know them; because we feel ashamed or harbor guilt, when we see them? We often fail to reach out when they are alive and well, or suffering; yet we don't hesitate to show up at a funeral to grieve, and to pay our respect. Despite who they were; or how they may have acted, they were in fact, family. Why not embrace and accept our family when we have the opportunity, before it is too late?

We have children that grow up and can't establish nor maintain a loving family of their own; because they don't know how to. They didn't grow up with an example of what a "family" is supposed to be. We have children that grow into adults that are confused when it comes to establishing a relationship with the siblings that they never knew they had. Why are there children that are being kept, a secret? We have children that grow up harboring anger and resentment towards parents and family members that want to establish a relationship with them; because they never knew any of these people. They were not there. We have parents who chose not to be there; and that want to be honored and respected as parents publicly. Many of these parents still chose not to be there, behind closed doors. We are quick to judge and tell someone else that they have issues or problems; because they have yet to get over their hurt and anger, yet we can't even get over our own! Why? The "truth" has yet to be faced, assessed, and addressed, in an effort to aid us towards our own personal healing.

Healing will take time; and that timeframe varies for us all. Healing can be a difficult process for many. Some people are ready; and others are not. Do not be afraid to put yourself forward and say," I'm sorry. I was wrong. I did not say, nor do what I should have done, I'm ready to make it right. I forgive you sincerely, and wholeheartedly." In order to grow and to move forward with the peace and freedom that is only attained through facing that odd, bizarre, confusing, weird, harsh, sad, painful, annoying, "truth" that only you know. You have to be willing to face, assess, and address your truth. If you need professional help in understanding how to do so; then do not be afraid to seek wise counsel as well as trusted advisors, who are supportive of you and that want to see your life change, in a positive way. You are not alone in your suffering and what you have to endure is not solely your problem; or issue. There are others enduring your struggle as well. There is nothing to feel guilty, nor ashamed about. Know that at some point; the joy, happiness, peace, and the freedom that you seek from letting go, is indeed for you. It can be yours.

There are people that you can talk to. There are those that understand. There are those that will encourage, and support you. You can become a better father. You will become a better mother. You are a better parent. You can let go of that painful past, regarding your family. You can move forward with your life. You can move in a positive direction. You can embrace, accept, and love your family and relatives for who they are. You do not have to wait until it is too late. **Strive to face, assess, and address your truth in order to embrace your ability to heal from within.**

Chapter 7
Love and Relationships

"I'm tired of trying to find someone who will love me for me, I give up! There aren't any good men and women out there these days. I don't know how to love, because I never received love as a child. I have a problem trusting people and that's why I can't establish a long-term relationship. All men and women cheat. Are there any honest people left in the world to love? I will never fall in love and marry again after what that person took me through! I'm just living my life for my kids and that's who receives all of my love. Love isn't real and doesn't exist; it's just fleeting emotion. Relationships just aren't for me; it doesn't matter what I do or how hard I try, they just don't work out."

Have you ever found yourself saying or asking yourself any of this? Do you know people that feel the same way? Why? Are relationships that difficult to pursue and maintain in this day and age? Is the fact that you did not receive maternal, or parental love affecting your relationships? Was that marriage so terrible that it has caused you to give up on the love that you desire?

Some of us are Blessed to have wonderful caring and loving relationships full of love, joy, and laughter. Then there are those of us who can say that building a great relationship takes work; yet it's all worthwhile in the end! **For many of us, when it comes to finding and building a stable, great, and healthy relationship; it's a struggle.** Many people have opted to give up on this struggle; and have simply decided to be alone. Then there are those who just keep on trying to make it work no matter what. Constantly enduring the ins and outs, ups and downs of love!

My question is, "why?" Why does your relationships seem to continue to fail, time and time again? Why do you continue to hold onto the hopes of finding that special someone along with everlasting happiness, and contentment? Why do you continue to struggle in the name of love? Is it that difficult to find the right mate? Are our standards set too high, or too low? Do we even have standards at all? **Are there any good men and women left out there; or are we all damaged and hurt to an extent by the past failures, shortcomings, and letdowns that we have all faced at some point in time?**

Let's take a look at a few scenarios:

Scenario 1- (Behind closed doors, a young woman struggles to find the love that she desires; and to maintain a fulfilling, and long lasting relationship. She is attractive, has a great career, owns her own vehicle, and is buying a home. She has no children. She considers herself as independent. She finds herself often attracting men that are not suitable for her. She attracts men who do not want to work a job, has few ambitions, sets unattainable goals, have emotional baggage from previous relationships; and they often end up "using" her for what she can provide for them. She has a good heart, and tries to help the men reach stability for themselves. She often ends up being let down. The men she dates, claim that she is too demanding; and that her standards are too high! The young woman witnessed her mother endure the "in, outs, and ups and downs" within various relationships with men that were not suitable for her, as a child. She grew up striving to never find herself within dependent relationships with men that are not good matches for her. The cycle seems to continue. The young woman now in her 30's, is debating whether or not to give up on finding a love that is for her, and opting to just date; as opposed to seeking marriage. She feels that there is no 1 out there for her. **Do we have men and women within this predicament amongst society today? Why do you think that it is so difficult for this young woman to find a man that offers what she has to offer in terms of "bringing something to the table? Would this woman be "wrong" for giving up on the love she desires at such a young age? How did the behavior of this young woman's mother influence her mentality and outlook on relationships as a child? What needs to occur for this woman to heal and develop a better outlook in terms of "love?" Are her standards too high and is it important to have standards when pursuing a suitable partner?**)

Scenario 2-(Behind closed doors, a man struggles to find a suitable partner to establish a worthwhile relationship with. The man is in his late 20's, and has made mistakes within his past in regards to life, career, education, and finance. The young man lives with his mother. He did not choose to go to college upon graduating high school; but instead, right into the workforce. The young man was in a relationship for a few years at 1 point, in which he has a child. He endured numerous ups and downs within that relationship; because it was with a partner that was not for him. They were incompatible in terms of "thought, speech, and action." That relationship took the young man through a lot of changes. When that relationship ended; the young man was in another relationship which lasted a year and a half. Another child derived from that relationship. The relationship ended due to the young man losing his job; and not making enough money to provide for his family, and pay child support for his previous child. The young man works a mediocre part-time job to help his mother with the bills. The young man does not know his father; nor does he have a relationship with him. His mother pacifies the young man. She makes excuses for the choices and decisions that he made previously, within his life. The young man dates occasionally; yet has a difficult time finding a suitable partner. The women that he date feel as though he is not ambitious enough, and look down upon him for living with his mother. The young man desires to enter college and to get his life on track; but the people he associates with are not supportive, nor encouraging. They tell him that he is better off staying with his mother. They do not want to see him doing better than them. His peers enjoy the young man being dependent upon them. Behind his back; they often ridicule him, and talk negatively about him amongst each other. The young man is debating whether or not to give up on finding a suitable partner. He uses drugs, and alcohol recreationally within his free time to cope with the poor choices and decisions, that he made early in life. **Are there people who endure this type of struggle within our society today? Is it too late for the young man to go back to school and get his life on track? Is his mother hurting or helping him by "pacifying" him although he is an adult? Why do you think that the women look down upon him when he tries to pursue a current relationship? Does this young man need to find some new people to associate with and call**

friends? Why? Are drugs, and alcohol a good coping mechanism when you are enduring "changes," within your life? What needs to occur within this young man's life in order for him to heal and move past his past and towards a better future? How do you think a father not being present within this young man's life influenced his decisions and choices?)

Scenario 3- (A couple has 3 children and they decide to marry. They marry and have 1 more child. They are happy. The husband and wife both work and make good money. After a few years; the wife loses her job. She decides to go back to college to further her education. All of the financial responsibility falls upon the husband. At 1st the husband happily obliges; but after a year, he begins to complain about having to pay all of the bills alone; and how he does not have money for himself. The wife is focused on graduating college; and so she ignores his complaints. The young man confides within his close friends and they try to encourage him; but somehow end up ridiculing him. His friends are divorced; and are bitter single parents who pay child support and alimony, to their former families. They tell him that he shouldn't have ever gotten married! Behind closed doors, the young man begins a clandestine affair with a co-worker; because he feels that he has no 1 else to relate to. He is prideful, and is ashamed to talk with his family members. His family members are not too fond of his wife; and think that she is using him to further her own objectives. The wife finds out about the affair, and the husband and wife separate. They remain separated for 5 years; because neither wants to pursue a divorce. They do not want to be together; for they are too bitter, and resentful towards each other. The wife tries to move on with her life; but can't find a man to take her seriously. She has 3 children, and is still legally married. The husband's affair ends in shame, and ridicule. He wants his family back. The wife is still bitter towards him, and eventually files for divorce. The 3 children take the divorce and the changes that they endure the hardest; unbeknownst to their parents. The man vows to never marry again. **Does this occur amongst our society today? What could the husband and wife have done differently to change the outcome of their marriage? Why did the man confide in "friends" whose marriages did not work out well for** them? Why was this couple afraid to confide in their own families about the issues that they were facing within their marriage? Does cheating often occur within a relationship when 1 partner feels that their needs are not being met? Why? Are children often the ones who are hurt and letdown the worst in a separation, or divorce? Why do you think that it took so long for this couple to pursue an actual legal divorce? What does this family need to do to heal; and to move forward with their lives in a healthy, and positive manner?)

Why does "Love" seem to become an internal struggle within our mind, when and if things aren't going the way we feel they should? When our partner is hesitant to give themselves fully on an emotional level; then why do we retreat and pull back? Doesn't this put a strain on what we are hoping to build?

Numerous books have been written about Relationships and how men and women can look within to find love. The 2 key factors that I feel many of us sidestep because we are so in need of a partner to love us is "compatibility," and have you fully "recovered" internally regarding your mental and emotional outlook; in order to move forward with someone new? "Compatibility;" as in do we think alike, share the same views, have the same goals, are we willing to work together, compromise, build each other, encourage, motivate, inspire? Are we willing to put all selfish needs and wants aside to come together in order to love? When I use the word "recovered," I mean have you fully moved on from the previous relationship? Have you healed from it, come to terms with why it did not work out, accepted and assessed where it or perhaps you went wrong, forgiven it, and let it go? Are you still hanging on in hopes that you or perhaps the other person will "come around?"

Are you waiting for them to call, drop in for a random visit, end the relationship they are in, mature, realize that they are missing out on the best thing that could ever happen to them? Do you still bring them up in present conversations although they are now a part of your past? If so, then you have not fully "recovered." This can be why it is so difficult for you to move forward and see clearly in order to embrace the "new" for what it is and what it has to offer?

The hardest thing about letting go is "letting go." Does this statement harbor truth? Of course it does; especially when you feel that you sacrificed and gave your all for the sake of loving that 1 person. Your family and friends told you that wasn't the 1 for you; but you ignored the warnings. You saw numerous signs before, within, and after the relationship. The "Signs" as to why it could not work out, and grow into something meaningful. You justified and continued to ignore the signs; because you were in "love." You felt that person made you happy. They made you feel whole, and complete. For some odd reason, they could never commit themselves fully to you. They claimed that they had been through so much in the past, within "relationships." It's hard for them to love completely. This creates "A struggle to love."

Does this make a person the worst person in the world; because they let you down? No, it means that they have yet to heal; and that you may not be the 1 to bring forth healing, and truth for them. It may take time, which could be months or years. It may take someone mistreating; or letting them down to see the error of their ways? If you continue to pursue a meaningful relationship in which you are the only 1 giving your all; and trying to make it work, then you will continue to be let down. This in turn will damage your outlook; and your chances of pursuing a meaningful relationship with a person that is right for you. **This is why it is so important to let go. In order to look back and assess where things went wrong and why. In order to heal and continue to move forward. Sometimes, it isn't always the other person; but ourselves that have yet to heal?**

Sometimes we move too fast; because we are so in need to have to have a partner to feel complete. If we were deprived of love as a child; then that unconditional love and nurturing that we missed out on is what we are always grasping for at every opportunity. Some people love the wrong type of people. Some people want to love everybody. Some people could care less about love; as long as their needs and wants are being met. Some people have yet to figure out how to love themselves, so therefore they are unable to love someone else. There are those of us, who seldom stop to assess where things went wrong and why. We pursue and endure current relationships, in a state of "confusion." This behavior in turn confuses their partner.

Is it ever okay to be discriminating, judgmental, picky, or to set standards? Some will argue about this based upon their own current standpoint, or condition. If you know what type of partner that you are looking for; because of what you tried in the past and saw for yourself, what could or would not work, then you know what you need. **I don't mean judgment, discrimination, or standards as in tall, fat, skinny, short, bald, rich or poor? I mean judgment, standards, and discrimination** as in knowing the value of your self-worth. If you are a clean, OCD, neat freak; you don't want an unclean or careless partner. Can it work? Is it possible to find a balance? Yes it can; but it will be a difficult and challenging relationship. If you are a goal oriented, ambitious, security conscious, caring, and giving person; then you are probably not looking for a carefree, free spirited, self- centered, lazy, spend-thrift. That will be a difficult and challenging relationship. If you have a job, pay your bills on time, a vehicle, and take care of your responsibilities; then you don't want a person who doesn't. That will be a challenging, and difficult relationship. If you believe in God, attend worship services, and your partner doesn't; it will be a difficult and challenging task to find a balance. There are numerous cases in which opposites attract; and make it work, through unconditional love. Some people are just too different to do so. That is okay. If you are seeking a peaceful balance that doesn't involve constant challenges; then it is important to set standards, be discriminating, and judgmental when pursuing the type of relationship that you are seeking to have, nourish, cherish, and develop.

How about building a relationship with people that have children? There are those of us who have children that state that, they would not date another person with children; because they don't want to deal with the drama, from the other parent. Some state that they would not; because they don't want to raise another person's child(ren). They feel that it is too much responsibility; and not their own to take upon. Some adults have yet to mature; and are not responsible, or stable enough to care for another person. There are those who don't mind stepping up to the plate for another person's child(ren) and becoming that absent parental figure, mentor, and role model for those children. They realize the importance of being present and active in not only the life of their partner; but their children. They are in the relationship to make a difference and to serve a purpose in the lives of all involved, for the better.

To love a person unconditionally means to not look upon the conditions; or the reasons as to why you can't love them fully, and wholeheartedly. It is important to assess whether a person takes care of their children from a previous relationship, if children are involved. Do they support them emotionally, as well as financially? Do they have a decent or great relationship with the other parent, in regards to the child's health and well-being? Do they visit and perform activities with the child? Do they care about the child at all? Are they neglectful towards the child? In most cases; if a parent takes care of and looks after their children despite whether or not the relationship that created those children worked out; then they will do the same for yours if you decide to have children with that person. We all know of exceptions where this is not always the case. It is important to assess the character; and motives of a person, if you decide to get involved with someone who has a child from a previous relationship. **Children are innocent and often become the victims of neglect, due to a parent's poor choices and decisions in regards to their well-being. Do not aid, excuse, or justify negligent behavior; yet seek positive solutions to better the situation as a whole.**

There are some people with children who harbor self-pity; because of their past faults, mistakes, or misdeeds. They may not know how to take a relationship seriously once the opportunity is presented; because they may have conceived a child or children, outside of a committed relationship. They may suffer from internal issues emotionally, when it comes to being in a serious relationship. They may have trust issues, infidelity issues, issues with being honest, and of having good morale. **It may be hard for them to believe that someone can love them wholeheartedly for who they are; because they may have suffered ridicule or judgment behind their situation. They may take these inner issues out on an unsuspecting person, if they have yet to heal**.

What about those "cheaters?" You know, the men and women that seem to always be "up to no good" as soon as their partner that they are in a serious committed relationship with turns their back? Why be in a serious and committed relationship if you feel the need or desire to cheat, and be with someone else? Why cheat? Some people state that, their partner's sex drive is not as high as their own; and that's why they cheat! Sexual incompatibility; yet you still choose to be considered seriously committed to 1 sole person? Is this an act of "selfishness?" Some state that, they cheat every time their partner upsets, frustrates, and angers them. They go to someone else who they feel appreciates them; but they always come back home. Some say, that's just what men do? It's in a man's nature to want to be with someone else? Is it in a woman's as well? Why? Why continue to hurt a person that continues to love and put their trust in you time and time again? Why continue to go back and forth constantly adding more confusion, and chaos? **Why struggle to be committed and even decide to marry 1 sole person; when you know that you have a problem with commitment, and have yet to heal?**

Is it possible for a "cheater" to have been letdown early in life by someone that they loved, unconditionally? Perhaps, they found out that person was cheating on them when they were giving their all just to be with them? They made up in their mind at some point in time never to trust a person again with their love. So once they enter into a new committed relationship; they will do well for a while, until they regress. They have yet to heal. The results often end in embarrassment, guilt, and ridicule. Some people just like having the upper hand over others, and some use it as a means of manipulating, and controlling a partner. This behavior is wrong. It is hurtful, and harmful. **The person who suffers the most in situations like this is often the person who was cheated on. They become the victim and by not healing; carry this damaged emotional pain, hurt, and baggage into the next relationship.** They may end up becoming the cheater, just to avoid the emotional hurt, pain, and letdown from a past they have yet to let go.

Having a healthy relationship with the right person can be a challenge. It can be a challenge to trust, be honest, to love unconditionally; and to give your all. Who knows who you're giving this

to; and whether it's all worth it, in the end? Some people marry and after years of marriage, decide that they just want to enjoy the single life; because of what they may have endured within that marriage. Perhaps, they were married to the wrong type of person. The will and desire to want to create a successful and happy marriage in spite of; kept them in a situation that was not good for them. Some people stay with a person for years waiting to become married. Once that relationship runs its course, and a marriage never occurs; they opt to just be alone. Why waste more time? Most of the time, we are just giving our all to the wrong person. It is our reluctance to let go of a bad situation for whatever reason; that poisons us mentally, and emotionally. This leaves us wounded and causes many to give up on a joy and happiness that we have deceived ourselves, into believing isn't for us. When do we decide to heal? Why is "healing" so important? **The time it may take for us all to heal, find ourselves and move forward varies because our situations vary.**

Take the time to find yourself after a relationship ends. Many of us become so focused on our relationship and the other person; that we often lose touch with our own goals, ambitions, dreams, and hopes. When that relationship ends we are sometimes left blowing like a leaf in the wind; alone and wandering until we come back down to earth. Understand that everything we set forth to accomplish in love, may not work out as we desire for it to. That is okay. You may have done some foolish things in love; but that doesn't make you a bad person. **Know that you gave your all if you did; and just because the person you were with did not appreciate or know how to accept it, it doesn't mean that there isn't someone out there for you who will give you their all.**

Avoid negative thinking. You are not defeated, until you accept defeat. There are instances in which both people need to separate in order to find themselves; and get their own lives together individually to benefit each other, as a whole. If I don't have my priorities in order and you do; then I can't benefit you, especially if I'm not trying to get them in order. It may take time apart for me to figure it all out and to get myself together. If too much time doesn't elapse and you move on; we may possibly be better suited for each other at a different place in time. Then again, we just could have been a bad match up; and did not see eye to eye in our views, goals, and ideals. A completely different person may be more suitable for you. If you've made up your mind to give up; and have accepted defeat, then you will miss out on that person. Develop a positive outlook and mentality about love and keep your heart open to the possibilities of finding the love you desire. **Timing is essential; and you want to make sure that your heart and mind are in the right place, when that time comes.**

Set, and reach your goals. If you've been searching for a better job that pays more and benefits your life and well- being, then go for it! If financial circumstances came between you and your love, then be open to growth and change. Money does matter and you need it to be able to provide even the simple things in a relationship; such as going out to dinner, or the movies. A person will eventually get tired of always footing the bill and feel like you are using them; and if someone else comes along that will take that load off, chances are you will get left behind. Better yourself financially, when you are alone to do so and can focus. If you want to go back to school, then do so. It takes an education to obtain a great career for many of us today. In the time that you will waste pursuing a "dead end" relationship; you can obtain a degree, and a career that will better your circumstances.

Avoid pursuing a relationship in which you are trying to better yourself; and your partner is not. They will hold you down, and you will end up wasting time and getting nowhere.

Envision yourself in a better predicament. When the damage is done; you only have yourself. Envision a better life for yourself than you had; and strive to let go of the hurt, and pain. **Remember that bitterness, and resentment is toxic. It poisons your ability to think positively. It hinders your growth as well as your ability to pick yourself up; and move forward with your life, in a positive direction.**

Learn valuable lessons from your previous mistakes, and letdowns. This goes back to taking "accountability." You are not accountable for what the other person did wrong to you; but you are accountable for yourself. You are accountable for what you say, do, and how you act. If you acted ignorant, childish, and immature; then work to correct this behavior. Think and act as a mature and responsible adult. Take accountability, and strive to become better. Many people say, that if they could do it all again; then they would do things differently. When a relationship ends, you now have a clean slate! This is your time for you to change your ways, and to correct your faults. Become a better you, for the next person. How can you expect different results with a new person; if you're still doing the same old things in action and speech? Make sure that you seek to build a relationship with another person whom has taken accountability for their past, as well.

Strive to become better, not bitter. What will make your life better, and healthier? Old habits can be hard to break. How do you grow and become better; when you don't see anything wrong with yourself? Do not always take offense to criticism. It can be seen and used in a constructive manner depending upon how you view the message. Some people judge the messenger and what's wrong with them; but everyone that you encounter, is not meant to become a permanent fixture within your life**. Some people are set in place for a season, to teach us something that we have been missing out on; or have failed to learn**. Allow others to help aid in your healing and growth. Do not build walls in which you hide on the other side of; always thinking that you are right, and the other person doesn't have a clue. This is a negative way of thinking. It hinders growth, as well as your ability overcome, your own personal challenges.

Avoid becoming shallow. Do not always look at what the other person has to offer you; or what type of background they come from. Focus on getting your own; and seek to find a person who has their own. You can both combine to have more; and not take away from the other's progress. Some people that look like they have it all together may not have anything at all going for themselves. Get to know a person for who they are. If they don't fit into your life in a meaningful manner, don't try to force a relationship. Some people make great friends. See the potential within a person; because we all have potential. A flower can't grow without sunlight or water. Seek to nourish others, if the opportunity presents itself. Make them better for themselves; or someone else if you can. **Some people see what we fail to see within ourselves; and can help us solve the toughest of problems, by coming up**

with valuable solutions. It's not always what you can gain; but sometimes what you can give. Avoid getting used. Do not overextend yourself.

Love yourself. When you can love, accept, and embrace you for you; then you will probably do a great job of loving someone else. See the beauty within; and embrace your struggles. Know that the worst things that have occurred within your life can only get better. Acknowledge where you have been and why in past relationships. Understand where you need to be. Seek the desire, and the will to find and embrace your greater self. That's the joy, peace, and happiness within. Leave the mess, stress, drama, confusion, and chaos behind! **Know that things will not always be perfect. Be willing to take a personal assessment of who you are.**

Strive to become a better communicator. We live in the age of the text message; and we all know how those little short and to the point messages can send signals of confusion? Whatever happened to just calling and talking to a person for hours? What happened to meeting up to chat in person? If you consider yourself an adult, then do what mature adults do; seek to successfully communicate your point. Do not write notes on the back of the envelopes that the bills came in; and leave them all over the house for your partner to stumble upon. This frustrates and confuses them, as to why couldn't you just say that?

Develop your ability to not just talk; but to listen and to understand the other person. If you don't understand, then ask them to break it down for you; or to specify clearly. Many people find a way to make it work and you know what works best for you. **Avoid hostile confrontation. Seek tactful and positive communication.**

When you can accept your past for what it was in regards to relationships; where you have been and why, then you are making progress. When you've changed as a person for the better; and no longer harbor anger and resentment as to what did not work out and why, then you are on your way towards healing. You are on your way towards forgiving the past. You can successfully move forward in pursuing and obtaining real and unconditional love. Healing occurs at different times and rates for all of us. **There are some people who choose to never face, assess, and address the truth regarding their past in** relationships. **These people continue to go forth often finding themselves with people and situations that are not good, nor beneficial to them.**

Be willing to admit your errors and strive to correct them. Strive to grow from the lessons that you have learned. If you learn from what did not work out; then it is possible that when the time comes again, you will know exactly how to make it work. Know that the love that you desire is for you. You can have it. Know that you are capable of letting go. You can move past your past. You can start over. You can and will, find a suitable partner. You are not "crazy." You are a good person. You are worthy of true, and unconditional love. There is someone for you. **Do not be afraid to face, assess, and address your truths in regards to your relationships. Be willing to embrace the healing within. Know that you are capable of moving towards your greater self; as well as a brighter future, that you deserve.**

Chapter 8
Children, Parenting, and Responsibility

"Do you know that your Father didn't want you?! Your Mother ran him off. I wouldn't go looking for a man or woman who wasn't there for me when I was growing up. Your mother is too busy living her life and doing what she wants to do; that's why she's not here for you. That man said that you are not his child and that your mother is lying on him. How will a man with 3 children who doesn't even want to work a job provide for them? If I were you, I would stop worrying about my parents and live my own life because they don't care about you! I don't understand why you continue to believe that man will help you raise that child when he hasn't done anything to help you, yet! I'm not your parent; but you should be glad that someone cares enough to want to raise you, because your family doesn't want you."

How many of us have heard these hurtful words or perhaps even spoken them to or about someone? How did this make you feel? Are you still dealing and coping with the issues that you faced as a child, now in your adulthood? Do you desire to know the truth about why your Mother or Father wasn't there for you? Are you willing to establish a relationship with them today? Is it too late? Have you yet to fully heal from the damaging effects taken upon your life? Why?

Where is my Daddy; a question that many of us who grew up in a single parent household with just a Mother or an acting parental figure probably asked at some point? Where is my Daddy; a question that many of our children and teenagers who grow into adults are still asking, yet today in this present time? Why are so many Men absent from not only the lives of our children's Mothers; but the lives of their own children? Why is it so easy for us to take part in acts of intimacy to create life; yet not become responsible enough, nor seem to have enough care and concern, to be an active parental figure over that life? Let's take a look at a couple of scenarios:

Scenario 1- (Behind closed doors, a young woman struggles to provide and care for her 2 children. She had the 1st child at the age of 16. She had the 2nd child when she was 22. The children do not have the same father. The young mother now 28; receives no help from the children's fathers. The parents of the young mother help her with the children when they can; but they tell her that having the children by "no good" men were her choice; and so she has to take responsibility. 1 of the children's father comes to visit the child randomly, on occasion. He is bitter because he has to pay child support. He opts to not keep a job so that he will not have to give the mother of his child anything to aid in the well-being of the child, financially. The other father claims that he doesn't know if the 2nd child is his and refuses to take a paternity test to find out. He feels as though he is justified in not being present within the child's life or assisting the mother, financially. The young woman works a full-time job and often does not have time for the children. She leaves them with friends to babysit while she works and goes out to clubs on the weekends. She feels as though she was deprived of the best years of her life; because she became a mother so early. She is not mature enough although she is an adult, to take accountability for her own actions. She blames the children's fathers for her struggles in life. The children love their mother; yet they suffer emotionally and often misbehave at school and when in the care of others. **Does this scenario occur within our society today? Is the mother wrong for not being willing to grow up and take accountability for her actions? Are the fathers justified in the way that they feel and act towards the children? Are the parents of the young woman wrong for telling her to take responsibility for her kids? What needs to occur in order for the people involved within this situation to heal and move forwards in a positive direction for the well-being of these children?)**

Scenario 2-(Behind closed doors, a young man neglects his 4 children. He has 2 by the same woman and the other 2 have different mothers. He claims that he does not make enough money to take care of all 4 of his children and to provide for them. He works a full-time job and does not pay any child support to any of the mothers. Instead, he buys the latest clothes, shoes, and owns 2 new cars. He lives with a roommate and pays half of the bills. When he is off work; he goes on dates with other women and spends money on them; often paying their bills for them if need be. The mothers of his children talk negatively of him to the children as well as others. When asked about his children; the young man lies and states that they are doing well, and brags about what he does for them; although he does nothing. The young man does not have a good relationship with his mother and does not know his father. He blames his mother for the struggles that he has in relationships with women and with his children. He feels that he would have turned out differently if she had been there for him when he needed her. His mother battles a drug addiction. The young man is 32 years of age. He does not reach out to his children and states that it is their mother's job to raise them because they wanted them. **Does this occur within our society today? Why do you feel the young man blames his mother for his negligence towards his own children? Why does the man pay for what he wants to; but doesn't provide for his children, financially? Is the young man justified in his speech and actions? What will possibly continue to happen within the life of this young man if an intervention does not occur? What needs to occur in order for the people to heal and move forward in a positive direction within this scenario?)**

So why is it important to be a Daddy, a Father? Why are so many men using the excuse that, "I didn't have a daddy, so I don't know how to be one?" Why do so many of our Women have "Daddy issues," and have a hard time establishing a secure relationship of lasting value with meaning and purpose with the opposite sex? Is it because so many of our children grow up facing the struggle of having to watch a single parent make a way for them; the best way that they know how? Are our "Parents" and parental figures teaching us that there are no good men out here today, because if there were, then men being "fathers" would not be an issue? Do we not have enough Men who are active parents reaching out to those who aren't and showing, teaching, and instilling in them through guidance and mentorship that there is a better way?

What are the struggles and issues of a person that grew up with an absent father? In this day and time there are just as many absent mothers, as there are fathers? You have women of various ages having children and giving them up not just for Adoption; but for other family members and friends to raise? There are instances in which a woman will have a child for the sole purpose of trying to keep a man; and when she learns that man doesn't want her or the child, she gives the child away and moves on with her life? How is this emotionally and mentally even possible?

What do we have to do to not just ensure the well-being our children's mental and emotional health; but the likelihood that these children will grow up to be mature, and responsible parents to their own children? Let's be honest……….. having a child, is not just a great responsibility emotionally; but financially. A question that many of us need to ask ourselves before we decide to create a life and bring it into this world is, "can I not just provide love and nurturing to this child; but can I provide for it financially?" Can I afford to buy diapers, milk, food, clothing, and pay daycare expenses? Am I financially stable enough to not just take care of and provide for myself; but for another? Do I have a partner that is willing to contribute to this child's well-being; or will I be alone? Will I be dependent upon family, friends, and others to help me and my child? We often hear of unprepared parents who came into parenthood unplanned or perhaps unknowingly state, "I made a mistake." A child is not a mistake; but not only a Blessing, but a choice.

When we decide to have unprotected sex and engage in acts of intimacy; whether we realize it or not, we are making a choice. What will determine whether or not that choice is a good or a bad one, is your own personal conditions. It is important to have stability, a job, reliable transportation, family, supportive friends, as well as a reliable partner. By having good conditions and foundations already set in place within your life; you may not have to endure such a great struggle, to raise and provide for a child. Everyone who has a child does not have the best circumstances.

Amongst our society today, we know that we have unwed mothers, unplanned pregnancies, deadbeat, absent fathers, and a host of other types of conditions that are considered, "not right." We have men that could care less about their own well-being; let alone that of a child. **Being a parent is serious business. We must not begin an individual cycle that starts with us; yet**

can ultimately create hardships, struggles, and issues for the lives of our children?

Many of us can attest to having a parent that was not there for us while growing up. We can attest to recalling important dates and times within our lives and looking around to not see the person that we wanted to make proud. We remember them not being there to share with us, within that moment. We can attest to making a vow to always be there for our own children; and doing whatever it takes to make sure that they know not only that we are their parent, but we love them. Many of us keep these vows and do just that. We are there. We go above and beyond to give whatever it takes, whenever we have to. Many of us stray from keeping our word. We fail to keep our promise to these children; because it is either too difficult, too demanding, or for unknown reasons. Some of us are not mature enough; or we just don't care. What is the problem?

There are instances and occasions in which a woman will not only try; but go out of her way, to keep a child from their father. Is it because the man and woman's relationship did not work out? Is it because the woman is selfish, self-centered, possessive of the child, jealous-hearted, nor does she want to see the child happy with no 1, other than herself? Did that woman have an absent father; and develop a mentality that men can't be depended upon, nor relied upon? Did her mother teach her to be independent and not to rely upon a man; and therefore she is unintentionally and unknowingly instilling this notion, within her child as well?

There are instances and occasions in which a man will tell the mother of a child that he will be there for them; and if he can't for "them," then he will for their child. When the mother asks him for money, in need of help and financial support for that child; the man gets angry, upset, ignores, and avoids her. He tells the child that he will come and get them to spend some time; or to take them somewhere, and do something nice with them. He doesn't keep his word. Yet, he is constantly spending money on himself or others; as if he doesn't even have a child. He is constantly bragging and telling others how he does so much for the child. How he is always there for them. In reality, he isn't. So why lie? Why pretend? Who does a lie justify?

Who does a lie protect? Apparently himself in his own mind; but if others know the truth, then it doesn't really stand. A lie, is still a lie.

We have to stop putting these children in the midst of these unnecessary struggles; that force them to take sides; and to choose who the better parent is. This is selfish, ignorant, and bizarre behavior. The only thing that it creates is confusion for the child. This leads to "issues" once the child gets older in age; and gains an understanding of right, and wrong. These same issues can possibly lead to the misguidance in how they treat their own children and partner, once they enter into adulthood.

So how do we heal? How do we move past these issues and struggles when it comes to being a parent? 1st, we have to stop blaming others for our shortcomings. If your father or mother was absent; then does this mean, that you have to be? We have to take accountability for our own actions, choices, and decisions. If you create a life with someone, then take responsibility. It is apparent that all relationships with great promise and potential do not work out; and sometimes end in divorce, separation, or estrangement. We see this in society every day; yet does an innocent child have to suffer?

Learn to work together to ensure the well-being happiness, and health of a child. It takes 2 people to create a child; so why can't it take 2 people, to raise that child? Some men and women get jealous when another man or woman enters the other parent's life? Why? This means that they will at some point interact with their child, as well. People move on with their lives when it comes to love and partnership. The choice to take care of your child, who was already present beforehand, should not be something to move away from.

Communicate effectively with each other as mature parents. Every time the mother and father of a child talk; it should not lead to an argument, or disagreement. Seek tactful and peaceful conversations. Keep in mind the sanity of the child. Who wants to witness a mother and a father that doesn't even live together or interact on a daily basis; constantly arguing, having a standoff, or confrontation every time they see each other? The life of your child should not be a chaotic life; because the child's parents cannot see eye to eye, communicate effectively, or work together. You have to put pride aside, and selfishness to rest. Raising a child is not a competition;

and should not be a challenge. Someone has to be the bigger person. Raising a child is no longer about you; but about the well-being, mental health, and sanity of that child, or those children.

Healing takes time; and that timeframe is different for us all, individually. Some people are bitter, resentful, and hold grudges; while others move forward, realize their faults, and work to correct them. Holding a grudge hurts no one; but you. The toxic poison weighs on your emotions, and mentality. It keeps you from progressing, and maturing. Learn to let go. Accept your own personal truths. Seek to correct past faults, and misdeeds while striving to become a better parent. If a mediator; or counselor is needed to move forward; then do not hesitate to seek professional help. Reach out to support groups, seek friends who can relate to your struggles.

Seek those who can help you overcome; and move past them, as well.

We all make mistakes in life; and have done things that we are not proud of, when it comes to specific relationships. There are words that have been said; and left unspoken. No child should have to live a life; and grow into adulthood questioning, "where were you, why you weren't there, and do you love them?" Seek and desire to be what you never had; if you grew up, with an absent parent. You of all people should know how that feels; and the toll that it took upon your childhood. Once you create a life, know that it's not all about you anymore. It's about ensuring that life does not have to one day look back; and question, "where was my mother, or father?" There are times when the hardest challenge can be the easiest thing to do. You may have to do something that was never done for you. When a child is born, there is no manual handed to you on how to raise that child up to be who; and what you, want them to be. We learn as we go; and grow, as we learn. Know that you can become a better parent. Know that you will take care of, as well as love your children. Know that you can heal; and move towards your greater self. Do not let what you did not have, prevent you from becoming what you can; and have to be. **Strive to face, assess, and address your personal "truths." Seek to heal from within; and become a better parent, in regards to your child, or children. They need you to set the example for them.**

Chapter 9
Religious Belief

"The reason that I don't go to Church today is because, all the "so-called" Christians are worse than the people outside of the Church! I was raised in the Church and when I became an adult; all I've witnessed is the same people contradict themselves in terms of religion. The only thing you will find in the Church is a bunch of hypocrites! I know people that go to Church religiously and all they do is raise hell. I don't believe in God, because if there is a God then why do so many bad things happen to good people? All I've ever heard is that Jesus is coming back; but I've yet to witness it so why should I believe? I'm always trying to do the right thing; but only bad things happen to me so I stopped believing!" **How many times have you heard any of these statements or questions randomly? Have you ever found yourself asking any of these questions or stating any of this? Why?**

Free will gives us the choice to choose. It gives us the choice to speak, act, and feel however we want to regardless of whether it is deemed "right or wrong." So what were you taught? How were you brought up? Were you raised in the Church? Did you attend Church religiously as well as actively participate within the Church? Were you taught to fear, love, and believe in God? Did you witness bad things or negative circumstances and encounters with others in spite of your beliefs? Are all people in the Church hypocrites, do they contradict themselves; of course not. So what led you to feel and believe that there is no God? What happened in your life that traumatized you so intensely that you decided to give up faith, hope, and stop believing in something greater than yourself?

How can we love God so much and believe in his power, might, and glory, yet continue to disobey and go against biblical teachings unintentionally and seemingly unknowingly? Why do we criticize and judge others so harshly? It is our struggle as human beings on this earth, to want to do the right thing even though we eventually make mistakes and do and say bad things. It is our struggle to be tempted, yet avoid temptation, to know what sin is; yet to ultimately wind up committing sin in its many forms. Why?

Although bad things continue to happen in the world; death, suicide, murder, adultery, fornication, jealousy, bitterness, resentment, wickedness, treachery, deceit, pain, suffering, heartache, lies, misery, and sadness, I still believe. I believe because I have witnessed and experienced the joy, happiness, redemption, power, glory, Blessings, peace, healing, and abundance gained through having faith, hope, and the belief in something greater than myself.

Why do we judge people that believe so harshly when we witness them struggle, when we see them backslide, when they make a mistake, have a fault, say something that we don't like nor want to hear because we feel as though they shouldn't say or do such things? Is it human nature? Is it because we see a mirror image of ourselves within others and our own struggles and find it easier to judge, criticize, scoff, mock, and ridicule others as opposed to taking accountability for our own actions, faults, and misdeeds? Is it because some people who consider themselves followers and believers of God sometimes come across as acting "holier than thou" in speech and action? Why is it that so many people who once made the same mistakes and led the same lifestyles as we do currently, judge and criticize us as if they were never where we are? Why do they seem to think that struggles and challenges are so easy to get over and face for everyone? Why is it as if we all will get where we need to be as human beings in terms of spirituality and religion; at the same moment in time? Let's look at a few scenarios that we all have had to face or endure at some point in time along our spiritual journey:

Scenario 1-(Behind closed doors, a young man begins a courtship with a young woman who has parents that are ministers within a Church. The parents object the relationship because they feel as though it is not of God and untimely for the young woman's life; although she is a young adult in age. The parents criticize and judge the young man harshly although they honestly know nothing about him for they only see that what they say and feel is right

68

based upon the fact that they are the young woman's parents. Emotions take over and the relationship endures. The parents soon become bitter and resentful toward the young woman for they do not see the error of their ways and are simply looking at the situation from not only a parental standpoint; but a judgmental standpoint as well. The young woman eventually becomes pregnant and the young man leaves her alone for he is not mature, nor responsible enough to take accountability for his actions and misdeeds. The parents disown the young woman upon finding out the news because she went not only against their wishes; but the will of God according to them. **Have you ever witnessed or took part in a situation such as this? Were the parents justified in their assessment of the situation and how they handled it? Can the young woman be held accountable for her faults and the consequences that arrived from her disobedience although she is a young adult? What could have been done differently to handle this situation? Does this occur too often within our society today?)**

Scenario2- (Behind closed doors, 4 children are taken into foster care due to their parents negligence. No biological family members step up to claim them. The children are separated and live in different foster homes; yet they all live within the same community and attend the same Church. Members of the children's biological families attend the Church as well. In Church the biological family members hug, embrace, and talk with the children. Outside of the Church, they have nothing to do with the children nor do they call or visit them as if they only exist within the Church. The children grow into adults and 2 of the children reach out to embrace and establish a relationship with the biological family members. The other 2 children are bitter and resentful toward them and consider them fake in their actions and speech in terms of how they claim to love and care for them; because of their failure to acknowledge and embrace the children outside of the church. **Are the 2 children who reach out to their biological family members justified? Are the 2 who chose not to establish a relationship wrong for how they feel although they grew up within the Church and understand Biblical teachings? Is anyone justified in their judgment and actions in a situation like this? Does this occur within our society today? What needs to occur**

in order for everyone involved to heal and move past the anger, bitterness, and resentment?)

Scenario3- (A young girl is raised within the church. She has prominent and active family members within the same church as well. When she becomes a teenager, she becomes pregnant as well as unwed. She continues to attend the church as well as take responsibility for her action and obligation as a single mother. Members within the church whisper negatively about her. They talk and gossip about her decision and how her family isn't as good and holy as they thought they were for if so; she wouldn't have ended up in that predicament. When she becomes an adult, she has yet another child out of wedlock and continues to be a single mother. Although she takes care of her responsibility and is a college graduate with an awesome career; people within the church still whisper about and ridicule her. She continues to attend the Church. **Is this behavior common in our society today within the Church? Are the gossiping Church members hypocrites because they pass judgment upon the young woman's decisions and choices in life? Is the young woman wrong for continuing to attend the Church services? What needs to occur for the people involved within this situation to heal and move past judgmental viewpoints?**)

We all have sinned and will possibly continue to sin at some point within our lives. I have sin and if you haven't; then you possibly may whether you realize it or not or do it unintentionally. We all fall short of the glory. Is this why so many people seek to attend a Church, harbor religious beliefs and teachings as well as believe in God? Do we all seek redemption; to be washed away and freed of our sins? There are those who chose not to believe in God because something bad happened to them that took away their innocence. There are those who chose not to believe in God because they were wrongfully accused, judged, mistreated, letdown, left alone, persecuted, abused, etc., Biblical teachings and scripture recite many of the things that occur in our society and world today. It was simply a different day in time yet; no one is free from struggle, adversity, challenges, and temptation no matter how sheltered they may be.

We hear of instances in which parents raise their children in the Church and as soon as they become adults and able to make their own decisions, they stray. Yet ultimately, once many mature and endure adversity they find themselves back in the church as active members and participants in their wiser old age. Why; perhaps, because they learned and became knowledgeable to the importance of building a relationship with God and creating a faith based foundation for their lives. **We as people often tend to yield to our own understanding because we have the free will to think, act, and do as we please. Once we become aware our faults, mistakes, and misdeeds, if we are wise then we seek to correct them.** We seek the "right" way. Many of us tend to mature and become accountable in late adulthood although we may have known all along in years prior the correct path to follow. We have a tendency to explore, rebel, fight, and go against Biblical teachings in the blind hope that we will find a better way of understanding how and why things work for us the way they do within our lives.

So when and how do we heal when we chose to follow God and feel as though we have been let down at times? What do we do when we put our trust in those who claim to be followers of Christ; yet something occurs in which we learn that they have deceived us? How do we get past judgmental members of the Church who smile in our faces yet talk about us behind our backs? How do we rise above all of the challenges that we face in and out of the Church? Will we ever find peace and harmony or will our lives continue to be filled with strife throughout?

When does our spiritual healing occur and how? For me personally, knowing that I believe in a powerful and almighty God that forgives me for the sin that I commit allows me to be willing to forgive myself as well as others for their shortcomings. Forgiveness is a part of healing. I have been talked about, looked down upon, mistreated, deceived, tricked, lied to and about, robbed, and I can honestly say that spiritually, mentally, and emotionally at some point in my life I have done this to others. **How is it possible for me not to be able to forgive a person and move forward in life when I believe in a God that forgives me and allows me to move forward because I believe?** If you have faults and you know what they are then how can you harshly judge others based upon their own? Nothing makes us "judge and jury" over the lives of others. We have to be accountable for ourselves in the way we treat people, carry ourselves, things we do and say, and how we act accordingly.

I can't tell you how to worship, who to believe in, when to believe, and why you should. There are many of us who claim to be Christians, followers of Christ, and believers, yet we do not carry ourselves accordingly. We do not hesitate to put someone down in speech and action; because we don't like nor do we agree with who they are, and why they are the way that they are. We may not agree with what they are doing. We may not understand why they are saying what they are saying. We may even question their motives and agendas for whatever reason? This is apparently human nature for better or for worse. **This is a part of having the free will to think, speak, act, and believe, in whatever we chose to**. Yet, does this make it "right?" Does this make what you do or have to say the "truth?" Perhaps, not in my mind but according to you it may be; and so that is your "truth," and you are held in account for it.

Know that there is power in the tongue. We do have the ability to hurt, damage, and cause harm to others in what we speak. **If you are always speaking negatively to or about someone then work on positive thinking and speaking.** If you are always lying and bearing false witness, then seek the truth as well as understanding and comprehending it. If you find joy in others sorrows and downfalls, then seek peace and ask yourself what if it were you in that predicament? How would you feel, what would you do? What would your reaction be? Learn to listen. Some people always feel that they are right and will use the Lord's name in vain to justify their speech and action. How are you saying and doing the right thing when you don't even know why a situation is like it is because; you care not to listen and seek to understand the situation as a whole?

Remember where you were and what you had to endure to get where you are. Everyone you encounter may not be on your level of understanding, or thinking. Someone may be closed or narrow-minded and can't fathom nor can they decipher why you are going through what you are going through. You know what you did wrong according to your situation and circumstances. You more than likely know what you will have to do to correct it.

Do not be afraid to learn a better way. You do not know everything because if you did; you wouldn't be in the predicament you are in. Develop an open-minded mentality and know that you are in control of the type of material that your "sponge" soaks up for better, or for worse.

Although you may stray or have strayed in your journey to become a believer and put into practice the teachings that you learn; know that it is never too late to start over, and develop a relationship with God. Your relationship is personal and there will be things that you encounter and experience that is solely for your learning curve in becoming a better person and getting on a better path, spiritually. You not only determine the foundation; but you set it. Someone may not be able to see your vision; or to understand it, when it is solely for you. Someone may not want to see you getting your life together and on the right track when it is solely your time to do so. Someone may not understand why you don't want to hang out, go clubbing, get high or drunk anymore, stop sleeping around, stop cursing, stop missing work, stop neglecting your spouse and children, stop avoiding your family, start making new friends, desire to go back to school, get a new job, move to a new house, and simply get your life in order when it is solely for you; and your benefit in striving to become a better person. It may not be for them to understand so stop expecting and anticipating them to. Your journey is yours and yours alone and along it you will meet like-minded people that are on the same page as you. Time will reveal whether they will be seasonal or permanent fixtures within your life.

In your journey along a path to heal spiritually, do not be afraid to let go. Do not fear moving forward. Seek those traveling the same path as you are to ensure that you remain along that path when you get weak, tired, and feel like straying. Be willing to embrace a new you. Be willing to embrace a change in speech, action, and demeanor; for the better. Allow yourself to be open to the benefits of closing the door to a path that was paved with despair, destruction, addiction, sadness, heartache, and strife! Be willing to unlock and open a door to joy, peace, happiness, prosperity, emotional and mental well-being, as well as positivity. Understand that you do not have to struggle alone. There are many people who understand what you are going through; and that are willing to help you along your journey. If they are not meant to be in your life; then time and circumstance will allow them to move out of it. The key is to learn and be willing to let go and not hold onto the negative people, places, and things once they have reached their "expiration date," within your life. Be willing to embrace a new you, and to embrace and face your truth in regards to your spirituality; for your healing lies within it. Know that you can, shall, and will overcome. Know that there is a greater self within you ready to emerge for the better. You can become a positive, and prosperous person. You can accept and embrace God. Do not be afraid to **strive to face, assess, and address your fears as well as your "truth;" as you seek to heal from within, spiritually.**

Chapter 10
Moving Past Your Past, and Towards Your Healing

"There is something wrong with you! You are still living in the past! Every time you talk to them, they are always going backwards; and talking about something that happened to them, a long time ago. That is over, and there is nothing that you can do about it. You need some help! You need to let that go! Why do you continue to let circumstances that are beyond your control hinder your progress? If it hasn't changed by now; then it will never change. You confuse yourself when trying to figure out how to solve problems that others have with you. Everyone else has seemed to move on with their life, except for you!"

Has someone spoken any of these words to you lately; or have you even said them to, or about someone? Why? What seems to be so hard about moving past your past, and letting go? Is it because it still hurts; and the pain, is relived every time you think about it, or someone mentions it to you? Of course it still hurts; and that is the reason why letting go is so hard, especially if you gave your all to make something work out for the best. You still suffer and endure your past pains, hurts, letdowns, and faults; because you had good intentions. You tried. You took a chance. You let your guard down. You surrendered yourself.

Some things that occur within our lives are simply traumatic. We have so many people within society today that endure the challenge of moving past their past, behind closed doors. Someone will do; or say something that they feel is right according to them at a certain point in time. They may be careless of whom it will hurt, or affect. They feel as though this form of behavior justifies them. This is a selfish act of deception. If you consider yourself a mature adult then why not address, and face the truth? It is understood that people make mistakes; and sometimes do and say things

75

that we are not proud of. We often end up regretting our actions, and words later. Why does it have to get to this point?

Inner emotional pain and turmoil eventually, becomes repressed anger. When we are angry and we get to a breaking point, then what do we do? We explode! We blurt out, and sometimes do things to hurt others; because we have yet to deal with, and cope with our own issues. We need some help! We need some intervention. We need some healing. **A sad fact is that there are many of us who choose to cope with our pain through the use of unhealthy mechanisms.**

We will experiment with drugs, and alcohol. Some eventually become addicted; and consumed by these poisonous, and toxic coping mechanisms. This behavior ends up hurting; and affecting not just our health and mentalities, but those around us. We will experiment with our sexualities; and cause ourselves physical and emotional harm, and abuse. This behavior leads to bad reputations. We infect and spread harmful diseases; all in the sake of thinking that we are finding an outlet to deal with our past pains, and hurts. Some of us will even take our anger out upon others; such as our families, friends, and children. This behavior often causes physical, mental, and emotional damage to them. Why? We have yet to address our own inner truths; and to move past, our past.

Is it easy forgiving? Is it a simple task to forget? Let's look at a few common scenarios:

Scenario 1- (Behind closed doors, a young man drinks heavily to cope with the fact that he had an absent father. He maintains what appears to be a normal lifestyle publicly; yet in the privacy of his own home behind closed doors, he often drinks until he passes out. In time he becomes careless to the fact that he is dealing with alcoholism; and begins drinking, and driving. He thinks that he is being cautious, and is getting away with this fault; yet his peers begin to notice. When he is sober, he tries to reach out to his father who lives within his community by phoning; or randomly visiting him. The problem is that a real relationship was never established. The father was never there; and so his actions are casual, towards his son. The relationship never perseveres outside of momentarily. The young man finds himself confused as to why his father seems to not care about him; nor wants to establish a relationship of lasting value? The young man continues his downward spiral, battling his addiction to cope and deal with his pain of feeling all alone. The person that he feels should care seems not to. **What will eventually become the outcome of this scenario? Does this young man have issues? Does he need some help? Is this young man holding onto the past? Are there fathers within today's society who behave carelessly towards their children, when they try to reach out to them? Why do you think this is? What can be done differently to positively affect the outcome of this situation?)**

Scenario 2- (Behind closed doors, a little girl is molested, and sexually abused by a close family friend. She wants to confide in someone and tell them what is happening to her, and how it is affecting her. Out of fear of consequence for exposing a truth that no one is prepared to accept; and deal with, she maintains her silence. The abuse continues into her teenage years until the family friend takes a job elsewhere, and moves to another state. The teenager now has emotional, and mental issues. She has yet to tell anyone. She becomes highly promiscuous, lost, and confused about love, as well as her sexuality. In adulthood she can't establish, nor maintain a healthy relationship with the opposite sex; because she has a problem deciphering the difference between love, and lust. She angrily blames her family for her problems. She constantly tells her mother through harsh words, that it was all her fault; and that she allowed this to happen to her! She feels as though she is now "messed up;" because of her mother's neglect, although she never confided the truth until adulthood. **Does this young woman have issues? Does she have a problem letting go of her past? Is she justified for feeling the way that she does towards her mother, and family? How does she move past her past; and towards healing, at this point? What should have occurred to prevent this situation from reoccurring? Is the mother at fault for not preventing what happened to the little girl? Does this happen within our society today?)**

Scenario3- (A young boy grows into adulthood as a foster child. He is determined to rise above his circumstance, and make something out of his life. He works hard in order to mentally, emotionally, and spiritually move past his hardships, faults, shortcomings, letdowns, and struggles. In time he eventually does; and is asked to speak at various community events about how he overcame the adversity within his life. Behind closed doors, he vividly and passionately recounts in detail things that occurred within his life; and how it hurt him. He feels as though he has yet to ever receive a simple apology from anyone that he felt wronged him. The peers he confides in tells him that he has issues; and has yet to fully move past his past hurts, and pains. Within the minds of his peers; if he has healed, then he wouldn't continue sharing and talking about the issues that are long gone. The young man feels as though he is helping others through sharing what occurred within his life; because he is letting them know that they can overcome the challenges, and adversity they face as well. He feels as though he has forgiven; yet it is hard to forget what actually occurred within his life. The strange realization that occurs to this young man is that his peers state that he has issues; yet they are constantly reciting things that occurred within their own past, that is no longer. **Does this man have a problem with letting go? Does he have a problem with forgiving? Is he wrong for sharing his story in an attempt to enlighten, and encourage others? Is he perhaps "preaching to the choir," and sharing with the wrong people; because they have yet to face their own truths? Does recounting; and sharing things that have occurred within our pasts, mean that "we have not healed" from them?**)

We all have a past. Our past is what contributes to our today; and often will, and can determine the outcome of our tomorrow. Letting go is extremely difficult for some people; because they care. They care about people; and the situations that arise with those people, that ultimately have a negative, or positive impact upon their life. Can it be said that those who simply forgive, forget, and move forward with their own life, don't care? Is it an act of selfishness for them to not care about how their actions can, and will hurt others? Does it matter if their actions have a negative impact upon their own lives? Is it true that our past defines us, whether what occurred according to us, can be considered the truth; or a lie? Does it matter, as long as we keep on living, and going strong?

When do we decide to heal? When do we take a stand; and decide to become responsible, and accountable? Not for what happened to us yesterday; but for what is occurring, today? At what point will we let go? We can't change; nor fix what happened to us way back then, because we can't go back in time. We can determine the outcome of whether or not we will continue to drown in self- pity. Often allowing our thoughts, and the questions as to why what occurred did. Why does the negativity; in regards to what we can't change, consume our minds and actions?

Why is your father's negligence keeping you from being a father to your own children? Why does your mother's drug addiction make you feel as though you need to seek those same drugs to cope; and deal with your own issues? Why does your friend's promiscuous behavior influence you to do the same; although you want a real genuine relationship? Why do you feel that since you lost that well- paying job with all those great benefits 3 years ago; that you are unworthy of another? Why do you feel that so much negativity and drama that you had no control over as a child; is now keeping you from experiencing the joy, peace, happiness, and prosperity that you deserve as an adult?

When do you determine, and decide that now is your time to move forward? Now is your time to Heal. If you need help or someone to talk to; yet you don't have anyone that is trustworthy to confide in, seek help through a professional counselor. Share your past pains and thoughts with those who want to see you doing better. Seek those that will encourage, and support you in your endeavors. Stop telling people who remind you of the worst times in your life; and that feed upon your misery and suffering, your business! Misery loves company; and someone who has yet to figure out why things are the way they are within their own lives, can possibly care less about you wanting to get your life on the right track, for you.

Face your truths. If you had an absent parent who was not there for you; and this is still affecting you in adulthood, then go to them to talk. Tactfully put the issues on the table to be addressed. If everyone considers themselves as adults in the now, then why not handle the issue; and the situation, like adults?

We all know that some people who did not do; or say what they should have at specific points in time, may not want to hear that now. They may feel that they let go; and have moved forward, in spite of. Is this even possible when the "truth" has affected you for the worse; and you have yet to find peace, since the other party is reluctant to address what actually occurred? It doesn't take an argument; or curse words to talk, through an issue. The parties involved need to maturely, and tactfully address the issue. Ask questions if you don't understand what is being asked; or said, in order to seek clarity. Your objective is to gain an understanding; as well as to reach a solution, or find a compromise.

Life is short; and we often wait until it is too late to say, "I'm sorry, I was wrong, I forgive you, how can I make things right, what will it take to move forward and past this hurt and pain?" How can we make things right; and if not "right," then better for all parties involved? A child is not to blame for a father choosing to not be involved within their life. A mother is not to blame for getting herself pregnant when it took "2 to tango," and create a life. A grandparent is not to blame for failing to properly raise you; and provide you with the wants that you felt that you needed, when you had a mother and a father who chose not to raise you. A foster parent is not to blame for letting you down by not allowing you to stay within their home, when they stepped forward to help you when your own biological family didn't. Your boss is not to blame for firing you from that job, that you wouldn't even show up for daily. Your family is not to blame; because you chose to sell, or do drugs as opposed to getting an education, finding a regular job, and now you are locked up. Your spouse is not to blame; because your marriage ended in divorce, when you refused to address, assess, and correct your own personal issues within that marriage. A social worker is not to blame for not making the best decision for your life; because you felt that they should have, when they were doing a job the best way they knew how. Your mother is not to blame for not helping you raise your children that you created through your own free will. **We as a people have to take accountability for our own**

shortcomings, faults, and mistakes. **We need to not blame what happened to us and why, on others. We must be willing to figure out how to right wrongs; and move forward in spite of how challenging, it will be to do so.**

In conclusion, Healing starts within. **Healing, and moving past your pain, hurt; and letdowns will start when you decide to take accountability for you.** You decide to make right your own wrongs. You decide to get your life on a better path. You must decide, and chose what will be the best move for you to make. If you have to relocate just to start over, then that is something that you must do. If you need to seek professional help in having someone to confide in, then you must do so for your sanity, health, and well-being. If you have "friends" that are keeping you down then you have to distance yourself from them; or let them go. They may feel as though you are "acting funny;" or that you think you are "too good." You are choosing to take your life back; and to get it on the right track.

You are in a process of Healing; and have to let go of the people, things, and places that keep you anchored to 1 negative spot. You know the things that no longer emotionally, physically, or mentally serve a purpose in your health, and well-being. It's called growing up, and maturing. If you have decided to live your best life, have a family, home, vehicle, career; and the lifestyle that you always envisioned for you, then you must move past the past, in order to embrace your greater self.

We often worry about what others will think; or say about the choices, and decisions that we make for our own lives. If you know within your heart that you are doing the best thing for you; then you must focus on that. Life has been hard and there will continue to be obstacles, challenges, and adversities to face. You have already overcome certain obstacles within your life. Why are you still looking, living, and moving backwards? Learn to forgive. Learn to let go of the issues; and the problems that you have overcome. Know that you are capable of starting over. Know that you can stop using, and abusing alcohol to cope with your problems. Know that you can stop using drugs to deal with your issues. Know that it is not too late to reclaim your life.

Know that you will find peace. Know that balance is yours. Know that your troubles will not last always. Know that you can develop; and build a healthy relationship with your children. Know that you and your spouse can work through your differences. Know that there is a career for you. Know that your financial struggles will end. Know that you do not have to continue to carry the burdens that once weighed you down; and kept you bound within the past. Do not be afraid to **face, assess, and address the truth about your past. Be willing to embrace the healing within that truth. Be willing to move toward your better life.**

Envision and become your greater self.

"If my name was God………"

If I was perfect…….then my name would be GOD. If I had money, then I would not be waiting on the check. If I had no flaws, then teachers, surgeons, doctors, lawyers, and counselors would not exist. However, since I am only human………I struggle each and every day to become a better individual. I will continue to strive to become a better mother, father, son, daughter, friend, spouse, partner, lover, worker, provider, and person in general. Each and every day for as long as I am breathing life; I will continue to learn, and to grow from the mistakes that I have made. I will utilize the lessons that I have learned, in order to correct my errors. I will strive to "face, assess, and address my "truths" in order to find the Healing within. I will lead a better life today; and tomorrow, than I did yesterday. I will no longer dwell upon my lesser, but become my greater self. I will heal. I can start over. I will not blame others for my shortcomings. I will take responsibility, and accountability for my speech, and actions. I will no longer dwell upon the negatives within my past; but embrace the positives within my present, so that I may have a brighter future. I no longer have to stand; nor hide behind closed doors, for they are now open.

www.ingramcontent.com/pod-product-compliance
Lightning Source LLC
Chambersburg PA
CBHW032102020426
42335CB00011B/460